Spirit Makes a Man

Spirit Makes a Man

By Joseph J. Panzarella, Jr., M.D.
with Glenn D. Kittler

DOUBLEDAY & COMPANY, INC.
GARDEN CITY, NEW YORK
1978

To my wife Josephine,
without whose faithful
and loving devotion and
determination I could
not have achieved what
I have.

Library of Congress Cataloging in Publication Data

Panzarella, Joseph, 1919–
    Spirit makes a man.

    1. Panzarella, Joseph, 1919–   2. Physicians—New York (State)—Biography. 3. Multiple sclerosis—Biography. 4. Physically handicapped—Rehabilitation. I. Kittler, Glenn D., joint author. II. Title.
R154.P2512A33   362.4'3'0926 [B]
ISBN: 0-385-12117-2
Library of Congress Catalog Card Number 77–11766

Foreword

DR. JOSEPH J. PANZARELLA (Joe to me) is a giant. The story of his life is not just a book—to me it is a cross between an epic (which is defined by Webster as a narrative poem recounting the days of a legendary historical figure) and a saga (which was first defined, in the twelfth and thirteenth centuries, as a tale of historical or legendary figures and events). Joe Panzarella's life story is eligible for both titles.

Joe Panzarella has had many honors including the Presidential Award in 1977 as the Handicapped American of the Year, presented in the White House by Mrs. Carter in the presence of a large audience of disabled and rehabilitation workers from all over the world and all of his family, children, grandchildren, relatives and also friends who came from afar to witness this moving spectacle. The award was received by his wife, Jo, and this was most proper for she and all the family were a team that made the day possible.

In a long life in medicine, I know of no patient or physician who has ever shown greater courage, fortitude, sensitivity, love and understanding. His wonderful description of his relationship with his beloved wife and family should be a solace and challenge to anyone in trouble.

This is a book that should be read by all professionals in the healing arts and the humanities and especially students in these fields. It should be available in patients' libraries, in rehabilitation centers, nursing homes, long-term care facilities, in homes for incurables, the dying and those fighting disease and disability.

We have a plaque on the wall of our reception room at our institute that to me sums up Dr. Panzarella's life best. It is the prayer of an unknown Confederate soldier, found in a churchyard of a cemetery in South Carolina. It has no title— our patients have titled it "A Creed for Those Who Have Suffered." It reads as follows:

> I asked God for strength, that I
>   might achieve,
> I was made weak, that I might learn
>   humbly to obey. . . .
> I asked for health, that I might do
>   greater things,
> I was given infirmity, that I might
>   do better things. . . .
> I asked for riches, that I might be
>   happy,
> I was given poverty that I might be
>   wise. . . .
> I asked for power, that I might have
>   the praise of men,
> I was given weakness, that I might
>   feel the need of God. . . .
> I asked for all things, that I
>   might enjoy life,
> I was given life, that I might
>   enjoy all things. . . .
> I got nothing that I asked for—but
>   everything I had hoped for,
> Almost despite myself, my unspoken
>   prayers were answered,
>   I am among all men,
>   most richly blessed.

The ingredients of this moving success story are simple but all powerful—courage, faith and love. It is a magnificent documentary of the life of a great man and a true physician.

Howard A. Rusk, M.D.
The Institute of Rehabilitation Medicine
New York, New York
September 1977

Spirit Makes a Man

I

It was like an invasion. From all corners of the country my relatives and friends descended upon Washington, D.C., that first week of May 1977. The reason was me. I had been chosen the handicapped American of the year by the President's Committee for the Handicapped, and President Jimmy Carter himself was scheduled to present the award to me. I couldn't have felt more honored had I been elected President of the United States myself.

It turned out to be a busy week, for President Carter as well as for me. At the last minute, President Carter had to go to London for a summit conference with leaders of the Western world. I figured that was more important than handing me a plaque, and so I did not mind, especially when I learned that his wife, Rosalynn, had asked if she could present the award. I was very flattered. The award meant a great deal to me, naturally, but what meant more to me was that the efforts of the handicapped to help themselves and to help others were being recognized at the highest level of the nation. Those of us who are handicapped need all the encouragement we can get and, more importantly, all the encouragement we can share.

Early Tuesday morning, May 3, my wife and I left our home at Setauket, Long Island, New York, by car. My car has a hoisting device by which somebody can lift me into the car or out of it. Ordinarily, we would have gone to Washington by plane, but I wasn't sure what my schedule would be, and I felt it would be better to have my car along rather than go through the ordeal of having people lift me out of my wheelchair and into cabs, then back again.

With us was our daughter Jacqueline, her husband, Richie, who was doing the driving, their new daughter, Farrah, and James, our fifteen-year-old son. We always call James our surprise package because he was born after we thought we weren't going to be able to have any more children. We left home early because I had an appointment at three that afternoon in Washington with Harold Russell, chairman of the President's Committee for the Handicapped. The first time I saw Harold was in a movie, *The Best Years of Our Lives*, in which he played the part of a sailor who had lost both hands in combat, which he had. The first time I met him was in 1962, when I was invited to Washington for a meeting of the President's Committee for the Employment of the Handicapped, and Harold was there. We had been friends and coworkers ever since.

It was a long trip, seven hours, with stops for the others to stretch their legs and for all of us to get something to eat. I had long before outgrown my reluctance to eat in public because of my need to have others feed me. That aspect of being paralyzed had become part of my life for years, and it no longer upset me to be stared at by people who wondered why a grown man had to be fed like a baby. Besides, I was on my way to Washington to receive an award from the wife of the President of the United States, and I knew there was nobody else in the restaurant who could say that.

At the same time that we were approaching Washington by car, our son Joseph, his wife Jane, with our new grandson Matthew Jeffrey were on their way by plane. My sister Lucretia and her husband and all five of their children were coming up from Virginia. Arriving the next day were my daughters Jeanine and Jennifer, their husbands both named Joe, and my granddaughters Lisa, Dana and Dawn, together with my mother-in-law, my wife's sister and husband, my cousins, friends from school and community, and my medical colleagues. Our congressman, Otis Pike, was also to be present. That evening our daughter Judy arrived by plane after having completed her classes at Cornell University.

I said to my wife: "Jo, maybe we ought to take up a collection."

She laughed. "I'd be glad to donate to it myself."

We all stayed at the Washington Hilton, where the award was to be presented on Thursday morning. A suite had been reserved for Jo and James and me—two bedrooms, a sitting room, even a kitchen.

Jo said: "I want you two to know something. I am not going to do any cooking while we're here, kitchen or no kitchen."

James was astonished. "Not even breakfast?"

"Not even breakfast," Jo said.

She didn't have to. Room service was excellent, and the hotel had evidently been designed with handicapped people in mind: there were no problems in getting around in wheelchairs; a lot of them were around that week for the presentation.

Harold Russell came to the suite at three. With him was William Sax, of the President's Committee for the Employment of the Handicapped. It was good to see them, and we had a pleasant visit. He gave me my schedule for the rest of the week. Fortunately, most of the appointments were in the hotel. Even so, I wondered how I was going to keep up with the schedule. After Harold and Bill left, the press interviews began. The reporters always wanted me to talk about myself, but I wanted to talk about the great deal that remains to be done to provide the handicapped better opportunities in life. That evening, the Panzarella clan, twenty-five strong, invaded the hotel restaurant and set a record for the amount of food consumed at one dinner.

The next day, Wednesday, was full of interviews—the press, radio, television. I had another meeting with Russell.

3

Then there was a cocktail party, and more interviews, followed by another Panzarella record in the restaurant.

That night I said to Jo: "I don't know how people who are always in the limelight can keep up this pace. I'll be glad when it's over."

Jo said: "You're loving it."

"I am," I admitted, "but I wouldn't want it on a steady basis. It would be an ego trip you wouldn't believe."

"I could believe it," Jo said. "I'm loving it too. The kids are so proud."

The next day was Thursday, the big day. We were told to be in the main ballroom by eight in the morning. As we arrived they were preparing the television cameras, the photographers were setting up, and people were already filing in. We were escorted to a reserved section which had been set aside for my entire family. This was up front and in mid-center. After the room filled to capacity and things quieted down, the United States Air Force Ceremonial Band began to play stirring music. Harold Russell and Mr. Rose, another member of the President's committee, announced the presentation of colors by the Joint Armed Forces Color Guard. Our national anthem was sung by Danny Scholl, a previous recipient of the Handicapped American of the Year Award. I was seated in the center of the aisle, with the spotlight on the flag and the representatives of the Armed Forces; and as "The Star-Spangled Banner" was sung, the flag swayed past my face. My emotions were so great that tears came to my eyes, and at that moment I was the proudest American in the whole world.

Following this, there was an invocation and some presentations, but we were scheduled to be in the hotel's Cabinet Room for the arrangements of the procession to the stage and to meet with Mrs. Carter. At precisely eleven o'clock, Mrs. Carter's personal secretary came in, introduced herself and set up the exact order of seating. Mrs. Carter then entered, surrounded by Secret Service men. I had seen Mrs. Carter on tel-

4

evision and pictures of her in the press, but I had no idea she was so attractive, so warm, so gracious.

Mrs. Carter came across the room to me and said: "Hello, Doctor. I'm so glad to meet you."

"I'm glad to meet you, Mrs. Carter," I said. "May I present my wife?"

Jo and Mrs. Carter shook hands. Mrs. Carter said: "You must be very proud today, Mrs. Panzarella."

Jo said: "I am. We all are. The whole family is here."

"That's wonderful," said Mrs. Carter. "Jimmy wanted to be here so much, but he had to go to London."

"I know," I said. "I'm happy that you were able to come."

She said: "I would have come even if Jimmy had been able to be here himself."

Jo startled me by asking: "Mrs. Carter, how is your new grandchild?"

Mrs. Carter beamed. "He's coming along beautifully. We all adore him."

Jo said: "My husband and I just had three new grandchildren within two months."

"Oh, my, that must keep you busy," said one of the busiest women in the world.

"It does," Jo said, "but we love it."

"So would I," said Mrs. Carter.

Then an official of the committee came up and told us we were ready to proceed. First the officials of the committee. Then the visiting dignitaries. Then the guest speakers. Then me. Then Mrs. Carter.

As the procession began to move onto the stage, I could hear the steady applause from the audience. Then we went out, my wife at my side, my son James pushing the wheelchair. I heard the volume of the applause go up, and I thought it was for Mrs. Carter.

James pushed my wheelchair to my place on the stage and turned me, facing the audience. The applause was deafening.

5

People were standing up all over the room. I glanced into the wings and saw Mrs. Carter standing there, waiting, the First Lady of the United States letting me have this moment to myself.

I looked out at the audience. I saw my children. I saw my grandchildren. I saw my relatives and friends who had come so far for this moment. I looked beyond them to the strangers —the blind, the deaf, the mute, the disabled, the retarded, the amputees—all there for the same reason, not just to honor me but to honor one of themselves, to share through me the promise which we each possessed: the potential of what we could make of ourselves. I felt a great love for all of them.

I thought of the people I wished could be there. My parents. My son Jeffrey. I was not too sure that they were not there.

I looked at my wife and said: "Babe, did you ever think that something like this would happen to a couple of kids from Brooklyn?"

And I remembered how it all began.

II

THE FIRST THING I NOTICED was that something was wrong with my vision. I was in medical school, studying hard under tremendous pressure. I was also in the Army. In order to get more doctors into the military faster, the Pentagon offered to pay for the education of medical students provided that, upon graduation, they would accept a commission in some branch of the service and serve four years. The catch was that I had to be willing to take accelerated courses, cramming three years of study into two, having already completed my first year. Even so, I thought it was a good deal. Attending medical school was making me a heavy financial burden on my parents, and I'd always felt uncomfortable about that. Now that the Pentagon was willing to pay the bills, it didn't take me long to decide to join the Army.

The routine was rugged. I was living at home, out in what was known as the City Line section of Brooklyn, and the Long Island College of Medicine was in downtown Brooklyn, miles away. I had to get up at five in the morning in order to travel by bus and subway to the college in time to report for an hour of close-order drill. Classes began at eight and ran through to five, with only a brief break for lunch. Then I had to report to the Army for an hour of military studies. After that I'd go to the subway station to meet Jo coming in from Manhattan, where she had a job as a receptionist-secretary. On the train, I'd go over my notes for the day and give them to Jo, and we'd go to our separate homes for dinner. Later I'd go over to Jo's and most often she already had my notes typed up. From Jo's I'd go home, study for a couple of hours more, often after midnight, and then I'd fall exhausted on my bed for a few hours of sleep.

This went on six days a week, week after week, month after month. So when the words on a page of a textbook began to dance in midair, I wasn't surprised. I knew I was working hard, perhaps too hard; but I had committed myself to the accelerated program, and the only way out of it was to quit school. I would rather have worked myself to death. All my life I wanted to become a doctor; and if I had had to submit myself to Chinese torture in order to get my degree and my license, I would have done so happily. Anyway, the printed words didn't dance for long. When I felt the condition developing, I would shut my eyes for several seconds and the attack would pass. I didn't tell anybody about it.

Then I noticed that something was wrong with my gait. My right foot began to drag. This was particularly noticeable during close-order drill. I had trouble keeping up and in step with the other men. Again, I decided this was merely the effects of working too hard. I didn't say anything about it. Next, there were periods when my right leg was so stiff that it was a real effort for me to go up or down stairs. Going down, I almost fell a couple of times. And yet I felt no pain. There were no other symptoms. With time, however, the symptoms I had became worse.

In the spring of 1944, I realized that I needed some medical attention. I went to the doctors at the college who usually treated the students and I told them what was happening to me. They recommended that I check into the hospital for some tests. I told Jo and I told my parents that the doctors just wanted me in the hospital for a few days of rest.

For three days I underwent every known medical test. When the results were in, the doctors still weren't sure what was wrong with me. I had apparently developed a demyelinating condition—the myelin sheaths which cover the nerves

8

had become inactive in certain parts of my body. It could be multiple sclerosis. Nobody knew what caused multiple sclerosis, probably a virus. Permanent remissions of the early symptoms were not uncommon. The alternative was the gradual increase of paralysis until it was total.

Jo came to see me that night. She asked: "Have they found out yet what's wrong with you?"

"They're not sure," I said.

She sighed. "All these tests, and still no one can determine what's wrong. Don't they have any idea?"

"Yes."

"What is it?"

I thought about it. Then: "Well, okay. I probably should have mentioned this to you before, but I didn't want to worry you."

"Worry me about what?"

"Honey, for the past few months my vision has been off. And sometimes my right leg is so stiff that I can hardly bend it."

"You're been working too hard."

"That's true, but it's not the reason for what may be wrong with me."

"What is it, Joe?"

"The doctors think I probably have some form of multiple sclerosis."

"Oh, Joe!" Tears filled her eyes.

"They're not sure, but that's what they think."

"When will they know?"

"It takes time. We have to wait and see. This may be as bad off as I'll get, so then everything will be all right. But it could become worse. Much worse."

"How much worse?"

"I could end up in a wheelchair."

"Oh, Joe!" Tears again filled her eyes.

Then I had to say something that had worried me all day. I said: "Jo, do you want to call off the wedding?"

"Don't be ridiculous," she snapped indignantly. "We've

9

been waiting for almost eight years to get married, and we're not going to let this change our lives."

"We could put if off for a couple of years," I suggested, "until we see which way I go."

"It really doesn't matter, hon," she said. "Nothing can change my feelings toward you, and we're going ahead with our plans."

I said: "Jo, don't let pride force you into this. People would understand. I would."

"I don't want understanding," she said. "I want to be your wife, no matter what."

I had to be sure. "Jo, chances are that in a few years I won't be much of a husband to you."

"I'll settle, just so you're my husband."

Now I had some tears. "I'm glad. I was so scared all day."

"You should not have been. When are they planning to discharge you?"

"I'm checking out in the morning. I'll go right to school."

"You're not going to take drill, are you?"

"No. I've been relieved of that. In fact, the doctors here are going to confer with the Army doctors about me, and I may get a medical discharge."

"Does that mean you won't get the commission?"

"I'll get the commission, but I'll have to give it up when I'm discharged."

"That's a shame. You were looking forward to it."

"I know."

"Have you told your folks yet?"

"No. I haven't told anybody except you. Jo, my folks will be here in a few minutes. Let's not tell them about anything just yet. They're both so excited about the wedding and the graduation and the commission. I don't want to dampen everything for them. I'll tell them later."

"All right."

Then my parents came into the room.

My parents came to America from Sicily, both coming from a small province of Palermo called Monte Maggiori Bel

Cito, but they did not know each other there. My father arrived in the United States in 1903 at the age of thirteen, making the steerage trip with his oldest brother, Mario. At first they lived in New York City with an aunt. Their hope was to save enough money to bring over their father, two sisters and a younger brother, their mother having died some years previous. My father's father had been an inspector of wheat for a wealthy family in Monte Maggiori Bel Cito, determining which wheat was to be exported and which to be sold locally. The job did not pay much and there was little future in it, so it was he who urged his sons to go to America for the better life.

At thirteen, with little education and unable to speak English, my father had trouble finding employment. He took menial jobs in factories and shops, saving all he could, learning English and educating himself. My father was never a greedy person. His only dream was to become independent and self-supporting. While working in a barbershop, where his duties were to keep the equipment and floor clean, he learned the trade by observing and practicing. He eventually served as an apprentice, and then he bought his own store in the Williamsburg section of Brooklyn when the original owner retired. The neighborhood was full of other people from Monte Maggiori. In time, my father and his brother were able to save enough to bring their family to America. They lived in the building where the barbershop was located.

My mother came to the States in 1908 at the age of eleven. Her father was a well-educated man. He had a beautiful handwriting and, in those days before the epidemic of typewriters, he worked as a secretary for a government official. Although the family was better off than many, they were not well off by American standards, and it was in search of a better life that the whole family planned to come over. The journey began in tragedy. While waiting to board the boat, my mother's younger sister darted into the path of an oncoming wagon and was killed instantly. The family decided that my mother's father should go on to New York, with the rest of the family joining him later after the funeral.

My grandfather could not find work in his field as a secretary and had to work as a carpenter. When my grandmother, my mother and the rest of the family came over, they had to seek employment in factories to supplement my grandfather's earnings. The family lived in the part of lower Manhattan that is still known as Little Italy, but when they heard about all the Monte Maggiorians living in Williamsburg they moved over there. My mother and father met through mutual friends. After they were married, they moved into an apartment above the barbershop. I was born in that apartment on February 21, 1919. A short time later, my mother's mother died in childbirth. My parents took into their small home my mother's father, the surviving baby and an older sister and brother. The place was crowded, but I remember it as being full of love and good times. One of my father's sisters married one of the Parisi brothers, who ran a butcher shop. They moved next door to the barbershop. About six months after I was born, they had a son, Russell. Russ and I grew up as close as brothers.

Dad wasn't making much. In those days a shave cost a quarter and a haircut fifty cents. But Dad had a good business. Besides the local people who came in for their weekend trim, Dad had a number of customers who were executives in factories in the neighborhood and who came in practically every day for at least a shave. Dad became friendly with these men and through them developed an interest in local politics. He never ran for anything and never campaigned for anyone, but he was interested in politics and liked to talk about it with his friends.

My father wanted me to become a lawyer. From the day I was born he would go through his earnings every evening and put the dimes in a special jar for my college education. But as soon as I was old enough to think seriously about a career, I knew that I wanted to become a doctor. It took a while to convince my father of this.

Eventually my father was able to buy the building where he lived and worked. But this was in the city, and my father had his eye and heart set on a place in the country. I was around five or six years old when my father's brother Mario bought a house in the City Line area of Brooklyn, and at the time the area wasn't built up much. My father and my uncle bought a parcel of land nearby which they cultivated into a farm. Every weekend my parents and Russ's parents drove us out to the farm and we'd have wonderful picnics as we worked on the crops.

One day my father saw a nearby house that was for sale. He was able to get a mortgage and he bought the place. The only thing I didn't like about the move was that it meant I would be separated from my cousin Russ. But a few months later, Russ's parents bought a house near ours. Then other aunts and uncles began buying property in the neighborhood. And my father kept talking to his Sicilian customers about the advantages of living out in the country. Before long the City Line section of Brooklyn began looking like a subdivision of Monte Maggiori itself.

III

My cousin Russ was my best man at my wedding. Jo and I got married on a Sunday in June, a week before I was graduated from medical school, the news about my health still a secret between us. Jo and I were supposed to get married at her church; but when we realized how many people wanted to attend the ceremony we got permission to move the wedding to my church, a much larger place. The assistant pastor of our church, Father Harth, was an old friend of the family. He grew up in Williamsburg and started getting his hair cut at my father's place when he was a teen-ager. When he happened to mention to my father one day that he wanted to become a priest, Dad stopped charging him for the haircuts.

Ordinarily, people didn't get married during a regular Sunday mass; but there was a war going on and people had to save gas, so Jo and I were married during the 11:30 public mass that morning and the people who were there didn't have to go to church twice that day. Then the bridal party went to a photographer's studio for the pictures. I had my commission at the time and wore my uniform for the ceremony, complete with first lieutenant's bars. I was very dashing. Then we all went to the Granada Hotel for the reception, the dinner and dancing on the roof. I had to report to the Army early Monday morning for another medical examination, so there wasn't time for a honeymoon. Jo and I spent our wedding night at the Granada Hotel. Next morning, when I reported to the Army, I was told to check into the hospital for a few days. I never had my uniform on again.

My cousin Russ has always claimed that he brought Jo and me together. Perhaps he did. We were inseparable as boys, except when we did something wrong and our parents wouldn't let us see each other for a while. That happened often.

Like most boys, Russ and I developed a love of cars at an early age. By the time we were ten we could stand at the highway that separated our homes and name the make, the model and the year of every car that passed. Rush hours were sometimes a challenge for us on the busy highway, but even then we scored high.

Our parents worried about us because of the highway. We had strict orders not to cross it when there was any traffic in sight and never to cross it during rush hours unless we were accompanied by an adult. We broke the rules practically every day. When we got caught, we weren't allowed to see each other for a few days. The person who caught us most was our Uncle Al. When his father and sisters came over from Sicily and settled in Williamsburg, Uncle Al took a job in Rhode Island for a year but then returned to live with the family in the apartment behind my father's barbershop. Then the Panzarella sisters began marrying the Parisi brothers and my parents got married and the kids started coming along. Uncle Al moved out of my folks' apartment and moved in with his married sister who eventually became Russ's mother. He lived with the family in Williamsburg and stayed with them when they moved out to the City Line. Uncle Al loved baseball. He would only take jobs that gave him free afternoons so that he could go to Ebbets Field whenever the Dodgers played home games. When the Dodgers were out of town, Uncle Al listened to the games on radio. The radio allowed him to wander about the house, and that was usually when he caught Russ and me on the highway. We felt safe only when the Dodgers were home. Sometimes we'd forget when they were out of town, and then we got into trouble. Uncle Al would tell Russ's father, who would tell my father, and then we'd go a few days without seeing each other. Otherwise, Uncle Al was very good to us, giving us money for candy or the movies or Coney Island, and we knew he was only concerned for our welfare and we loved him. Uncle Al never married, so he never had sons of his own; but in many ways he was as close to Russ and me as our own fathers.

Loving baseball, Uncle Al considered himself a good judge of baseball players. One summer Russ and I were on a neighborhood team, and Uncle Al used to come and watch us practice and play. He didn't think much of the team. "Maybe you should practice more," he suggested one day, "though I'm not sure that would help much. You play like you never saw each other before."

"We practice enough," Russ said, and he was right. We were practicing so much that I was getting a little bored with the game.

Uncle Al said: "I think you're just not good enough. I tell you what. I'll get together a team of men who never played ball together before, and I bet we beat you."

"You're on," we said.

A couple of days later, a team of men and team of boys gathered at the empty lot where the games were usually played. A coin was tossed, the men won and they chose to be up first. I was the catcher for the boys' team. Uncle Al was the first man up. He swung at the first pitch and sent the ball deep into right field. I cringed. Was it going to be that kind of game?

Uncle Al would have had an easy single, but he tried to stretch it into a double. The right fielder had a good arm, and the ball reached second just as Uncle Al did and hit him on the head. Uncle Al blacked out and dropped to the ground. We all ran to him. Somebody said to get some ice, and one of the boys ran to a nearby store for some. We applied it to Uncle Al's head, but he already had a lump bigger than the baseball. Dazed, he didn't argue too much when the boys insisted that he would have been tagged out anyway. He left the game and sat on the side lines.

The next man up was my cousin, who had just finished his medical internship, and he sent a line drive into center. It would have been an easy double, but he tried to stretch it by going on and sliding into third. His howls of pain filled the air before the dust settled. We all ran to him. You didn't have to be a doctor to see that he had broken his leg. Somebody called for an ambulance.

That was the end of the game. Uncle Al and Russ and I went back to Russ's house. When we entered, my aunt said: "The game over already?"

Uncle Al said: "Called on account of accidents." He pointed to the lump on his head. "Look at this."

My aunt looked. "How did it happen?"

"I got hit by the ball."

"So the game was called because you got hurt?"

Uncle Al said: "No. Doc Joe broke his leg sliding into third."

My aunt laughed. "Fine bunch of men you are, letting boys turn you all into basket cases."

"We did it to ourselves," Uncle Al insisted proudly, and the next thing I knew we were all laughing. My cousin, who had just opened an office, began his medical career by seeing his first patients with his leg in a cast.

Russ and I were still around ten or eleven when my parents gave me an Erector Set for Christmas. For months we spent hours putting together all the structures in the instruction book; then we put together some Rube Goldberg designs of our own. One day that summer Russ said: "Joe, why don't we build us a car out of the Erector Set?"

"How can we do that?" I asked. "We don't have any wheels."

"I know where we can get some wheels," he said. "There's a baby buggy in the basement of my house that hasn't been used for years. We can take the wheels off the buggy."

I looked at him. "Will that be all right?"

He shrugged. "We'll find out sooner or later if it is all right."

So we waited until the Dodgers were home and we went over to Russ's house and helped ourselves to the buggy, taking it over to my house. My father enjoyed working with wood, and he had an excellent workshop in the basement. We used his tools to get the wheels off the buggy. Then we carried the body of the buggy a few blocks away and left it in an empty lot. After that, we went looking for orange crates. Between the wheels, the orange crates and the Erector Set, we were able to put together a pretty good car. When we weren't working on it, we hid it in a storage shed in my basement that was seldom used. Also while working on it, we broke a few of my father's tools, and they ended up in the empty lot too. When my father complained about his missing tools, Russ and I avoided looking at each other.

When the car was ready, we checked the Dodgers' schedule, and on a safe afternoon we took the car outside to test it. I'd push Russ a block and then he'd push me a block. It was a lot of fun, and we were proud of ourselves. We also found out that it was even more fun to use the car on the highway than on the sidewalks. The smooth macadam allowed us to go faster and coast farther and there were no problems with curbs. We were having so much fun that we forgot about the Dodgers. One evening Uncle Al told our parents that he had caught us playing in our car on the highway. Surprisingly, we weren't punished for wrecking the baby buggy. The truth came out about my father's tools, and we weren't even punished for that. The real threat of punishment was in the fact that we had taken the car out on the highway. We had to give our fathers our solemn promise that we would never do that again. And we didn't. For about a week.

One day Russ and I noticed that the Dodgers were going to play a double-header the next afternoon. Good. That would take Uncle Al out of the neighborhood. The next morning, however, there was a very heavy rain, and it didn't occur to us that maybe the games would be called off because of a muddy field, which they were. That afternoon, the weather clearing, we were having a great time taking turns in the car, roaring up and down the highway. All of a sudden Uncle Al stepped out of the bushes directly into the path of the car, Russ at the controls. He was able to brake the car in time to stop it inches away from Uncle Al.

Uncle Al was furious. He said: "Get out of that thing." Russ got out. Uncle Al picked up the car by the front axle and pulled it around to the back of the house. Then he got a hammer and in minutes he totally destroyed the car, even twisting the buggy wheels so that we could not use them again.

Russ said: "I think we're in trouble."

I said: "I know we are. I'd better go home."

I went home, sweating out my father's return, the phone call from my uncle and then my execution. My father came home, the phone call came, and when my father hung up he looked at me, his anger smoldering in his eyes, he said: "You will not be with Russ for a month." I would have preferred the execution.

My father was a calm and quiet man. He enjoyed his family and his friends and his woodworking. He also enjoyed reading and he became, I suppose, a self-educated man. I don't remember any serious argument between my parents. I don't remember that my father ever struck me or my sister. My father could emit a loud, piercing whistle that I could hear blocks away, and I knew it meant that I had to head home immediately, regardless of what I was doing. My mother was more emotional, mostly out of her empathetic love for people. If you had a toothache, it hurt my mother more than it hurt you. The only time I had any problems with my mother was when I made up my mind that I was going to become a doctor. The City Line section wasn't built up much in those days, so there were plenty of open spaces where I could catch snakes, and there were many ponds full of frogs. I would take the animals home and dissect them in the basement, using my father's old razors as scalpels. If for some reason I couldn't complete a dissection, I put the animal in the family refrigerator. Next time my mother opened the refrigerator door there would be a scream that shook the house, and then I would really catch it from her. After this happened several times, my father said: "All right, if you want to be a doctor, be a doctor, but don't do any more operations around here until you get your license."

In those days teen-aged boys didn't have any money to take girls out on dates. For dates we had to depend on house parties, usually given by a girl. Living across the street from my family was a friend of my Aunt Mary's, named Catherine, who was in my age group. Her house had a big basement and Cathy was allowed to throw a few parties a year there, on her birthday, usually, and on certain holidays. Cathy had a party at Halloween, 1933, and everybody had to come in costume. I went as Li'l Abner. At fourteen I was already rather tall, so I figured that showing up as the muscular hillbilly would be just right for me. Also at the party was Josephine Seminara, Cathy's cousin from Brooklyn, dressed as a gypsy. I saw right away that she was very pretty, and as the evening unfolded I saw that she was a very good dancer. Cathy announced that we were going to have a balloon dance. The girls and boys were supposed to pair off into couples and we were to have a balloon tied to each foot. The idea was for the couples to keep bumping into each other, trying to break each other's balloons, and the couple who were the last to have all four balloons intact were the winners. Josephine and I won. I think the reason we won was that I was too big for the boys to want to bump into too hard and Josephine's balloons were hidden under the long skirt of her costume and nobody could see them. It was a lot of fun.

It was also for the purpose of being with girls that Russ and I and some of our friends organized a club. The makings for the club already existed. As the Monte Maggiorians started making some financial advances and moving out of Williamsburg, they also started drifting away from each other. They didn't want this. Like all immigrants, the Italian-Americans were proud of their roots and wanted to keep them. To keep them, my father and my uncles and many of their friends formed what they called the Society of the Sons of Monte Maggiore. It was a good organization. Once a month the members met in the upstairs dining room of Joe's Restaurant on Nevins Street in downtown Brooklyn. They'd have a business meeting and pay their dues and then have a big Italian meal, after which they'd break up into small groups and go to each other's homes to play cards or just to visit and to keep the roots alive. If a member of the society needed some money to expand his business or start a new business or to pay some sudden bills, he didn't have any problems borrowing the money from the society, repayable in modest amounts and at a modest interest. The society had a doctor on its payroll, a doctor who made house calls for fifty cents and took care of members when they had to be hospitalized. The society paid most of the bills.

So when my friends and I told our fathers that we wanted to form the Society of the Daughters and Sons of the Society of the Sons of Monte Maggiore, our fathers were delighted. We held our meetings on the same nights our fathers did, in the same hall, after our fathers left, the hall already paid for. First we had a brief business meeting during which we paid our dues. When we saw how much money we had, given to us by our fathers, we sent downstairs for hamburgers and Cokes. There was a juke box in the hall. We spent the rest of the evening dancing.

We decided that the social highlight of our year would be a cruise to Indian Point on the Hudson River Day Line. All the boys got dates, as did I. But meanwhile I had signed up to go to Plattsburgh, N.Y., with the Citizen's Military Training Army. I was to be away for one month, but I would be back in time for the cruise. During my stay in camp, I wrote to many of my friends and also to Jo. Her replies were so entertaining that I found myself looking forward to them.

Life at camp was hard but we all enjoyed doing our chores,

even peeling potatoes. My stay was made even more enjoyable when I was selected the outstanding basic trainee of our division. I also had fun on the rifle range, where I was able to win a medal as a marksman. I can remember my parents making the trip to camp and being very proud when I was presented the awards by General Drum at a full dress review.

When I returned from camp, I was given the sad news that my date could not make the cruise, and I had looked forward to it so eagerly. The cruise was the next day, so I had to find a date in a hurry. Suddenly I remembered my correspondence with Jo Seminara. I called her and invited her to come with me on the cruise. At first she was a little reluctant because it was such short notice, but I finally convinced her and she accepted.

I had a very good time. I discovered that not only was Jo pretty and nice and a fine dancer, but she was also bright and interesting to talk to. She asked me a lot of questions about myself—my life, my plans, my ambitions, and I did most of the talking, which may have been why I had a good time. Later, when I got home, I realized that I probably was the only son of the Sons of Monte Maggiore who didn't get to kiss a girl that evening. I didn't mind. I really liked Jo. I acknowledged to myself that it would be all right with me if I never dated another girl.

And I never did.

I thought about these things that Monday morning as I waited in the Halloran General Hospital on Staten Island for the Army doctors to start their examination. When they started, I found out that medical science had more different physical examinations than I remembered or imagined. I was tested most of Monday, all of Tuesday and Wednesday. Jo came to visit me every evening, but I had no news for her. Thursday morning the doctors gave me the news. Multiple sclerosis. Prognosis: uncertain. Immediate medical discharge.

I called Jo at work, and I asked: "Babe, can you get off early today?"

"I guess so," she said. "What's up?"

"They've finished the tests. I can leave. Would you mind going out to my folks' place and get me some clothes?"

"No more Army uniform?"

"No. I'm out, except for the red tape."

"Do they know what it is, Joe?"

"Multiple sclerosis."

She didn't say anything.

I said: "Jo, I don't want to face the family just yet—yours or mine. There's a big War Bond rally in Times Square this afternoon. Let's go there."

"All right," she said. "I'll be at the hospital as soon as I can."

It took her two hours. I was scheduled to start my internship the following week at St. Mary's Hospital in Brooklyn, but in view of my emotional state and the fact that I hadn't had a honeymoon, I called the doctor in charge of interns and asked for some time off. He was understanding and told me to report in two weeks.

When Jo arrived with my civilian clothes, I dressed and we took the Staten Island ferry to lower Manhattan and then the subway into Times Square. The place was so crowded that we couldn't see the stage and could hardly hear what was going on.

I looked around. I said: "I wonder if we can get a room in a hotel?"

"I don't know," Jo said. "It's difficult these days. Besides, we don't have any luggage. People might get the wrong impression."

We went into a Woolworth's and bought a cheap suitcase and filled it with books and toothbrushes and other personal things. We were able to get a room at the Claridge Hotel, a room that overlooked Times Square, and we were kept awake practically all night by the noise and the music and the lights from the all-night bond rally. We felt as though we were in the middle of a fish bowl.

23

IV

I HAD HOPED TO BECOME A GYNECOLOGIST. But now, faced with such an uncertain future, I was reluctant to make any plans until I had a better idea of what was going to happen to me. I had told the doctors at St. Mary's Hospital about my condition—at least the condition that was suspected, and they suggested that I start my internship and worry about the multiple sclerosis if it ever began to act up.

The day after Jo and I spent the night at the Claridge we went first to her house and then to my house to pack some clothes. I borrowed my father's car and we went to a resort hotel in Connecticut for what we hoped would be a two-week honeymoon. We were there three days when my mother telephoned: The Army wanted to see me right away on a very important matter. We returned to New York first thing the next morning and I went directly to Army headquarters. The very important matter was that I had to sign the payroll so that I could get my separation pay. I think it was twenty dollars. We blew it on lunch.

I said to Jo: "Babe, I don't think we're meant to have a honeymoon."

"It looks that way," she said. "What do you want to do?"

"Maybe I should get started on the internship."

"Maybe you should. We'll have to find a place to live."

"Yes. Let's try to find a place near the hospital."

"All right."

We did better than that. There were five of us interns who were going to work at St. Mary's, three of us married. The residence for interns was just across the street from the hospital. At the time hospitals—especially Catholic hospitals—were cool on the idea of accepting married interns—they would always be in a hurry to get home. But the three of us went to the administrator of the hospital and pointed out that if we were allowed to move into the residence with our wives St. Mary's would have intern coverage around the clock. It worked. It meant saving the cost of an apartment and that Jo's salary could go for food instead of rent. I was making only twenty-nine dollars a month.

I loved St. Mary's. Interns were given a fully rounded course, working in every department, learning more about medicine, learning more about ourselves. I was still attracted to gynecology, but I also enjoyed every other kind of work I was assigned to do. Every day was full of excitement for me. Each morning, as I headed across the street for work, I could feel the anticipation rise in me. I was becoming a doctor. I was learning how to help people. I was fulfilling my boyhood dreams.

Unless I was under pressure, I usually went back to the apartment for dinner. Jo turned out to be an excellent cook and a very prudent shopper. I was always amazed by the feasts she could provide on our meager incomes. Evenings when I was off duty, we would invite a few other off-duty interns in for poker, the evening brought to an end by one of Jo's banquets of snacks. My cousin Russ, who became a used-car dealer after the Army, usually invited himself.

Russ and I could never figure out why we always seemed to get into trouble whenever we got involved with cars. There was the car we had built ourselves when we were small boys. And there was another car when we were both around sixteen, the age when most boys become very much aware of girls. You didn't have to be a Sherlock Holmes to observe that the boys who had the most girl friends were the boys who had a car available to them. Although we both had permits to learn to drive, we didn't have licenses to drive without the company of a licensed driver. We had two cars available to us—my Dad's car and Russ's father's car. My father's car was housed in a garage next door to our home and could not be taken without being seen. My uncle used his car only on Sunday. The rest of the time it sat in a garage around the corner from the house.

One day Russ, his eyes sparkling with mischief, said to me: "Wouldn't it be great if we could get my father's car and go out to Coney Island and pick up some girls and take them for a ride to some nice, dark place?"

"It sure would," I said, "but you know your father would never let us have his car."

"He wouldn't have to know," Russ said airily, testing me.

I sensed the challenge. "He wouldn't? And how would we pull that off?"

"We could just take it."

"He'd kill us."

"He wouldn't have to know."

"You said that. But how do we keep him from knowing?"

Evidently Russ had already figured this out. "Well," he said, "I usually find out during dinner what my folks are going to do in the evening. You know they don't like to go out much, except over to your place. Mostly they have company come in. Well, we'll just wait until my parents have company some evening, then I'll get the car keys off the hook in the kitchen and we'll take off."

"Your father will hear you start the car," I pointed out.

"No, he won't. I won't start the car in the garage. We'll push it down the alley and into the street and down the block, and I'll start it there."

"Your father will kill us."

"Are you chicken?"

That did it.

The next evening Russ and I and two friends gathered in his backyard. His parents had company, so we knew his father would be busy in the front of the house. Russ went into the house and got the car keys. Then we all went to the garage and quietly hoisted the exit door. He got into the car behind the wheel and the rest of us got behind the car and pushed it silently out of the garage to a safe distance. Then I went back and closed the garage door. All of us then safely aboard, Russ started the engine, and off we went to Coney Island.

The car worked like a charm. We didn't have to walk around Coney Island for ten minutes until we found some girls who were more than willing to go for a ride. Our plan was to get the girls to some nice, dark place, and the girls probably knew that too. Whenever he headed toward a park or a deadend street, one of the girls would think of somewhere else she wanted to go. Then one of the girls suggested: "Why don't we go someplace and get something to eat?" That was bad news. Among the four of us, we boys maybe had a dollar. But life was cheaper in those days, so we were able to get hot dogs and Cokes for four. And we realized that the car was going to bankrupt us if we kept picking up hungry girls.

At the end of the evening, we dropped the girls off at their subway station and headed for Russ's house. About half a block away, he stopped the car, I got out and went to the garage and opened the big door. Then I stepped back into sight and gave Russ the all-clear wave. He revved up the motor, sending the car forward at a good clip, and when he was about twenty-five yards away he cut off the engine and let the car coast quietly back into the garage. Then we shut the door, Russ put the keys away on the hook in the kitchen and when the four of us were gathered again in the backyard we just stood there grinning at each other proudly. We had beaten the system.

After that, Russ and I and usually another friend or two helped ourselves to the car a couple of evenings a week. Always the procedure was the same, push the car out of the garage and let it coast in.

One night we had dates with some girls who had asked us

to take them to a dance. We had readily agreed—until we found out the price of admission. It was the kind of money we could never raise in such a short time. But we didn't want to stand up the girls. On the evening of the date, we took the car and headed for Coney Island. Just before we got there, we pulled up, and I put bandages on everybody so that we could tell the girls we had all been injured playing football and were in no condition to dance. We arrived looking as if we all had broken arms or sprained ankles or cracked skulls. The girls were sympathetic and settled for a drive, but when we asked them for another date they said we should wait and look them up again after the football season. That was the last we ever saw of them.

After several weeks of this, we were again heading back to Russ's home and, as usual, I got out first to go and open the garage door. When I opened the door, there, sitting on an orange crate in the middle of the garage, was my uncle. My heart stopped.

He asked calmly: "Where's the car?"

I said: "Russ's got it."

"Where is he?"

"Down the block."

"What's he doing there?"

"Waiting for me to give him the signal."

"What signal?"

"The all-clear."

"Go ahead and give it to him."

"All right." I stepped out where Russ could see me and sent him a halfhearted little wave.

Russ told me later that he thought something was wrong. Nevertheless, he revved up the motor, came forward at a good clip, cut off the motor and glided quietly into the garage. He was so shocked when he saw his father sitting there that he forgot to step on the brake until he was an inch from the man. Russ got out of the car.

As Russ got out of the car, his father said to me: "You go home. I'll call your father later."

28

I went home and went into my room and pretended to be reading a book. About ten minutes later my father came to the door. He said: "You and your cousin can't be together for the rest of the summer."

It was a very boring summer.

Even when we got older, cars seemed to play a role in our lives. During World War II, Russ served part of his Army duty at West Point and became familiar with the area. When he got out of the Army, Russ went to work as a used-car dealer at the time I was in internship at St. Mary's. One day Russ suggested that we all drive up for dinner at a seafood restaurant he knew near West Point. His date was Loretta Izzo, a nurse he had met through Jo and me. I was all for the dinner drive, but I was concerned about Jo. She was very much pregnant with our first child, and I didn't want her to exert herself. She told me she felt fine, so we took off, Russ driving.

We were driving along a country road near the restaurant when we came upon an old beat-up car going in the same direction but chugging along slowly. We got close enough to see that the driver was an elderly man. Russ tooted his horn a few times, but the man didn't pick up speed or move aside. Finally Russ gave a real blast on his horn, pressed on the accelerator and we passed the man. We had just settled in front of him when we heard a siren. I looked back and saw that old car moving up on us fast. The old man put on a state trooper's hat. So we had been trapped—a typical small-town trick in any part of the country.

Russ pulled up. The old man pulled in front of us. He got out and came to us and said: "License and registration."

As Russ produced both, he asked: "What's the charge, Officer?"

"Reckless driving," the man said. The hat was the only evidence that he was a policeman. He had no gun, and he was wearing a sports shirt and slacks.

Russ said: "But I wasn't going fifty when I passed you."

"Maybe. But you passed me in a no-passing zone."

"I didn't see any signs."

"They're there." He finished his note taking and returned the license and registration. "Okay. Follow me. You'll have to appear before the justice of the peace."

We followed him into a small town and pulled up in front of a store that had been converted into an office. While the girls waited in the car, we went inside with the policeman. I saw a desk, a couple of tables, a few chairs. The policeman pointed to some chairs on the far side of the room. "Sit there," he said. On that another elderly man came out of a back room. He and the policeman went to the desk and spent several minutes filling out three or four forms.

Then the second man said: "Approach the bench." We approached the bench—the desk. The man said: "You are charged with reckless driving. How do you plead?"

Russ said: "I didn't see any no-passing signs."

"They're there," the man said. "You'll have to stand trial. Bail is set at a hundred dollars."

We glanced at each other. We didn't have a hundred dollars to our names, let alone on us. Russ asked: "Can't we just pay the fine and go?"

"You'll have to stand trial."

I asked: "When will that be?"

"In a few days."

Russ asked: "And what do we do in the meantime?"

"Put up the bail or go to jail."

I said: "Your honor, I'm a doctor, and I have to go on duty at midnight. Is there any possible way you could release my cousin so he can drive me to work? It's his car, and there's no other way for me to get back."

He glanced at his watch. "There's a train in an hour. You can go, but he stays."

I started to get mad. "I'm not leaving without him. He's coming with me."

"Then pay the bail."

Russ said: "But we don't have that much with us."

The man asked: "How much do you have?"

30

We took out our wallets and combined our resources. I said: "Seventeen dollars."

The man glanced at the policeman, and I saw the policeman nod. The man said: "All right. You can pay the rest later. And be here for trial Monday morning at ten o'clock, sharp."

When we got back to the car and told the girls, we were all furious. It had been a shakedown, no question about it. We were lucky we didn't have any more money on us. We wondered how many times a day those two pulled this trick on people.

Russ said: "Now we've got a new problem. How are we going to pay for the dinner?"

Jo and Loretta each had a few dollars, but hardly enough to pay for a dinner for four. Jo said: "Let's go back to the apartment. I've got plenty of food for dinner. I've lost my appetite, anyway."

So we went back to Brooklyn and had dinner in the apartment where Jo and I had recently moved in my parents' house. Early the next morning, around four, I woke and noticed Jo was not at my side. I went looking for her and found her taking a shower. She explained that she was beginning labor. I immediately started giving her orders to hurry and get ready because we had a good half-hour drive to the hospital. I called my parents and told them what was going on. Finally, after what felt like hours, we started for the hospital. On the way, I was so nervous that I went down a one-way street in the wrong direction—and there at the corner was a patrol car. After explaining my confusion to the disbelieving patrolman, he finally got out of the car, went over and looked at Jo, then said: "Follow me." We had a police escort the rest of the way.

Later that day, after the baby was born, I called Russ and told him it was his fault that the baby was born two weeks ahead of time. He laughed and said: "You're lucky the baby wasn't born in a county jail."

It was a beautiful baby girl and we named her Jeanine,

after my mother's mother. She was born on June 9, Russ's birthday, and Jo and I decided to offer him the nicest present we could. We asked him to become Jeanine's godfather.

It was later that summer, late one night, when the phone rang. The hospital. I was needed immediately to give anesthesia at emergency surgery. I washed and dressed quickly and rushed out of the apartment. As I was hurrying down the stairs, my right leg slipped from under me, and if I hadn't grabbed the railing I would have fallen headfirst down the stairway. When I recovered, I inspected the stair. There was nothing on it that might have made me slip. I looked at my shoe. Nothing. Carefully I went down the rest of the stairs to my car and drove to the hospital, a certain fear in my heart.

After the surgery, I went home and back to bed. That morning, while we had breakfast, I said nothing to Jo about what had happened on the stairs. I said nothing about it to anybody when I returned to the hospital. Afterward, I went to the doctor who was in charge of the interns and I told him.

He sensed what was on my mind. He said: "Well, Joe, you were probably groggy as you went down the stairs. After all, you had been pulled out a sound sleep."

"I was wide awake."

"Maybe there was something on the stairs. Maybe your foot got caught on something."

"No. I checked. I think we ought to do some tests."

He nodded. "I'll make some calls. Four o'clock this afternoon?"

"All right."

So once again I went through a battery of tests. Because of the late hour, the appraisals weren't done until the next morning. My certain fears were verified. The multiple sclerosis had progressed. I was losing the strength in my legs.

The doctor said: "This could be as far as it goes, Joe."

"I know that," I said, "but I also know it can go farther."

He asked: "Does your wife know?"

"She knows I've got M.S.," I said. "She knew that before

we got married. But she doesn't know about the other night. I'll tell her now, of course."

"Good. Tell her not to worry."

"My wife doesn't worry. She accepts. I'm the one who worries."

"About what?"

"About how far this thing is going to go. About what happens if it goes all the way. About how do I support my family. About what happens to my work as a doctor."

"You shouldn't worry either, Joe. Take it as it comes."

That night I told Jo everything—the stairs, the tests, the results. She took it all as I knew she would—attentive, concerned, loving, but no tears, no dramatics, no pity for herself or for me. Acceptance.

And she said: "I think you should tell your parents. They have a right to know."

"Yes," I said. "It's going to be tough, telling them. I think I can talk to Dad about it without any problems, but my mother will fall to pieces. You know how proud she is of her son 'the doctor.'"

"Don't underrate your mother," Jo said. "She's a strong woman."

The following Sunday, Jo and the baby and I had dinner with my folks. Late in the afternoon, Jo and my mother were in the kitchen putting the finishing touches on the meal and my father and I were in the backyard on deck chairs having a drink when I decided that the moment had come. I said: "Dad, I want to talk to you about something. There's something wrong."

He looked at me. "You and Jo getting along all right?"

"Yes. It's perfect. It couldn't be better. It's not Jo. It's me. Dad, I've got an illness."

"What is it?"

"I've got a form of multiple sclerosis."

"What is that?"

"Well, the scientists aren't sure yet, but they think it is caused by a virus that attacks the nerves."

33

"Then what happens?"

"Gradual paralysis."

He was stunned. "You're going to get paralyzed?"

"I don't know yet. It's too early. But it's possible, and I thought you should know."

"Does Jo know?"

"Yes. I told her before we got married."

"You had it then?"

"Yes."

"And you said nothing about it to your parents?"

"I didn't know then how bad it was. I still don't know how bad it might become."

"Can't the doctors do anything for you?"

"No."

"What about you? Can you still be a doctor?"

"I'm going to be a doctor for as long as I can."

"And then?"

"Who knows?"

"Do you want me to tell your mother?"

"No, Dad. Not yet. I'll tell her. But not yet."

"She'll take it very hard."

"I know."

"She'll start praying for a miracle."

"That's what we need."

V

MY MOTHER always had a devotion to St. Joseph. When my football injury put me in the hospital and so close to death that I was given the last rites, my mother promised St. Joseph that if I lived she would honor him every year on his feast day by having a big party for poor children. I lived. After that, each year as March 19 approached, my mother would start baking cakes and pies and cookies, and she would call up churches and schools and orphanages to get the children. On the nineteenth the house would be full of children who, at some point, would sit down to a massive Italian meal, even when there wasn't an Italian child in the crowd. My mother kept this up as long as she lived.

As for me, I have had a devotion to the Infant of Prague for many years. I don't know how it started. I suppose that at some point of my life I faced a serious crisis or an important decision or a tough test at school, and I asked the Infant of Prague to help me. Whatever it was, it evidently worked out all right, and the devotion continued.

When I felt the time had come for me to talk to my mother about the multiple sclerosis, I asked the Holy Infant to help me in what I expected to be a very difficult experience. As it turned out, I didn't need the help. When the conversation began, I got the feeling that my mother already knew. Maybe my father had told her. Maybe she just knew. I never found out.

Now that the subject was out in the open, there were a few tears by both of us. And then my mother said: "Don't worry about it. I'll ask St. Joseph to take care of you. He always does anything I ask."

All I wanted from St. Joseph or the Infant of Prague or God himself was to be able to function, to find a place for myself in medicine and to be able to support my family.

Over the years, my becoming a doctor grew as important to my parents as it had always been to me. Actually, I came close to not getting into a medical school in the first place. As my high school career was ending, my parents and I agreed that I should do my premedical studies at St. Francis College. The college was close to our house, so I could live at home, and, more importantly, its tuition and fees were within the family budget. The day I matriculated, my father dug into the dimes he had been saving for years for my education, and we went to a bank and had the coins turned into more manageable folding money. My father was as proud as I was about beginning my premedical studies.

I grew to love the college. Because the school was small, there were better opportunities for closer relationships between the students and the faculty. Some of the priests and brothers teaching at the college became my lifelong friends. We still correspond with Brother Leo, my math teacher, and with Brother Pascal. Also because the school was small, the average student had more opportunities for extracurricular activities. I went out for practically everything. I loved sports, and I usually made the intramural teams I went out for. Again, because the school was small, the only sport in which we could compete with other colleges was basketball, and I was never good enough to make the varsity team. Even so, I wanted to be part of the school's basketball team, so my school chum Ralph D'Ascoli and I organized a cheerleading squad. I was already a rather tall and muscular young man, and I knew I wasn't cutting any dazzling figure during the cheerleading; but I was loud and I was enthusiastic and I was having a lot of fun. We had free admission to all the games, both at home and away, and those at Madison Square Garden. Jo always attended the home and the Garden games.

The archrival of our school was St. John's University. St. Francis never had to be ashamed of its basketball record; but St. John's was a bigger school with better teams, and it gnawed at us that we were seldom able to beat their basketball team. St. John's mascot was a cigar-store Indian which was displayed on the campus and taken to games for luck. One night before another game against St. John's, several of us went over to their campus and kidnaped the Indian. We left a ransom note, made out of newspaper headlines, stating that we would return the Indian only after the St. John's team, dressed in mourning clothes, made a public apology to the St. Francis student body in the school's assembly hall for having beaten us in the past. The event caused a lot of publicity in the New York papers, and we heard that the St. John's players were seriously considering making the apology and had even contacted the authorities at St. Francis to set up the assembly meeting. Then we heard that the St. John's team was planning on kidnaping the best player on the St. Francis team and holding him in hiding until the Indian was returned. We had some important games coming up and couldn't afford to be without our best player, so one night we quietly returned the Indian, and that was the end of it. There was some criticism about all the hoopla over the kidnaping of a wooden Indian by some crazy college students but we felt that kidnaping the Indian wasn't as crazy as eating live goldfish or raiding sororities or jamming a lot of people into a telephone booth. Anyway, at the next St. John's–St. Francis game, St. John's didn't bring along the Indian and St. Francis won.

Jo was almost as much a part of my college life as I was. She typed up all my lecture notes. I could have made a fortune selling carbons of the notes to my classmates; but I didn't feel right about that, and so I just passed them around.

It was while I was in college that Jo and I realized we were in love and that we wanted to get married. My father sensed what was on our minds, and one day he said to me: "Joe, your mother and I love Jo like she was already a member of the family. But remember that you have a lot of years in school ahead of you. I can afford to support you as a student, but I can't afford to support you if you get married and start having children."

"I know that, Dad," I said. "Jo and I have discussed it. We're not going to do anything for a while."

"That's another thing," he said. "Remember that Jo is a nice, Catholic girl. Don't try to do anything until you get married."

Maybe it was to avoid succumbing to anything that Jo and I kept ourselves so busy, mostly at the college. Whenever there was a dance coming up at the college, or a banquet or a seminar, Jo and I were always the first volunteers to set up whatever it was. I became active in many student activities and eventually became editor of the yearbook. Jo was always there to type up the articles, help with the layout and proofread the copy. When I ran for membership on the Student Council, it was Jo who listened to my campaign speeches again and again and showed me what I was doing wrong so I eventually did it right and won. Whenever I became secretary of some club or student activity, it was Jo who did the secretarial work. Because I loved the school and was having such a good time, my studies came easily for me. I was elected to the Duns Scotus Honor Society and I made the Dean's List twice. When, in May 1942, I received my B.S., it was *cum laude*. Each year the Ladies Auxiliary of the college gave a purse of twenty-five dollars to a senior for service and loyalty to the school. That year I got it. It should have gone to Jo.

Throughout college I tried to help cover the expenses of my education. Every Christmas I worked at the post office. Summers I worked in factories and stores. Whenever Jo and I went out on a date that was going to cost money, we always went Dutch. Living at home, I didn't have any board and

High school graduation, January 1934.

Joe (at left, age twenty) with his cousin Russ Parisi and a friend.

Joe and Jo's engagement, June 1943.

Joe and Jo after the wedding cermony at St. Fortunata's Church, Brooklyn, June 17, 1945. (Credit: Photograph by J. J. Steffel)

At the Third Inter-American Congress on Physical Medicine and Rehabilitation, Guatemala City, 1957, Joe gave a paper on the treatment of spasticity. (Standing right, Dr. Julio Castillo. Seated next to Joe is Dr. William Schmidt. Standing behind Dr. Schmidt is Mrs. Howard Rusk, Mrs. Castillo and Josephine. Dr. Howard Rusk is to Joe's left with his hand on Joe's shoulder.)

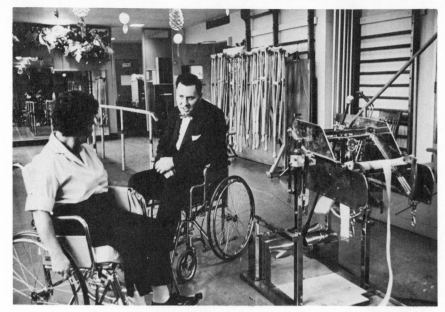

Counseling a patient at the Institute of Rehabilitation Medicine, New York University Medical Center, 1962.

The Panzarella family at the American Medical Association Convention, Miami, Florida, 1963. (Josephine and James are with Joe in front. In the back row from left to right are Jennifer, Jackie, Jeanine, Jeffrey, Joseph, Judy, and Joe's mother and father.)

room expenses, and with a mother who enjoyed taking care of clothes I rarely had to buy anything new.

The summer after I finished college I got a job in the laboratory of a chemical company in Manhattan. It was interesting work, but I was glad that I wasn't going to do it for the rest of my life. And then it began to look as though I might.

As students usually did, I had applied to several medical colleges, and my plan was to go to the best school that accepted me—at least the best I could afford. I hadn't been accepted by any medical school by the time I finished college; and as the summer began to unfold, I still wasn't accepted. I was getting very worried. Jo and my parents kept assuring me that good news would come along soon and that I should stop worrying. But I couldn't stop. I couldn't relax. The daily mail became a source of anguish for me.

Then one day I received a letter from the secretary for the faculty of the Long Island College of Medicine in Brooklyn. It was dated July 7, and it said:

"I am pleased to advise you that you have been accepted for admission to the first-year class in the Long Island College of Medicine. This class began on the 6th of July so it will be necessary for you to report at this office tomorrow morning at 9 A.M., and pay the fees which amount to Fifty dollars (Matriculation fee) and Two Hundred eighty-five dollars (Tuition fee for the first installment of the 1942–43 session) or a total of Three Hundred thirty-five dollars. Please advise us at once of your acceptance or nonacceptance in order that the place in the class may be filled."

I was elated.

I also went into shock.

I knew my father didn't have anywhere near that kind of money in his dimes collection and I had no idea where he would get the missing amount. My heart was in my mouth as I handed him the letter. He read it, nodded, then said: "I'll be back in an hour." And he left the house.

He was back in an hour. And he had the money. I found

out later that he had borrowed some of it from Uncle Al, the rest from a couple of friends in the Sons of Monte Maggiore. At the same time, my mother took a job in a war plant to help meet expenses. The next morning I was at the medical college down on Henry Street and I was able to pay the fees. I learned that the sudden vacancy had occurred because another applicant had applied to several schools and had decided to go to another school that had accepted him. I wished him luck for the rest of his life.

So I settled down to what I expected to be four years of very hard work learning how to become a doctor. Because of the Army's accelerated program, it turned out to be three years of incredibly hard work. There were times when I felt I could not get through another day. Not only were the intellectual pressures like mountains upon me, but the physical demands of keeping up the pace of being a medical student and a soldier at the same time were crushing. I don't remember ever falling asleep in a class, medical or military, but there were many evenings when I'd be waiting for Jo to type up my lecture notes and she'd have to wake me up to send me home, home not to more sleep but to hours of more study. Somewhere along the line, I evidently encountered multiple sclerosis.

During my internship, the question of a future residency often came up. My colleagues and some of the staff men offered suggestions for me in view of my illness. One day I found a note in my mailbox from one of the surgeons. He wanted to see me. In his office, he asked: "Joe, have you thought about going in anesthesiology?"

"No, I haven't," I said. And I hadn't.

He said: "Last night I had dinner with a friend of mine who's on the staff at Mary Immaculate, over in Queens. He said the hospital has a residency open in anesthesiology. They're looking for applications. Sounds like a good setup. And there's probably a staff assignment after the residency is completed."

I wasn't sure. I said: "Let me talk it over with my wife. Can I see you this time tomorrow about it?"

"Better still," he said, "if you decide you want to look into it, why don't you get in touch with my friend directly? I don't know how many applications they're receiving. You shouldn't waste any time." He gave me the man's name.

During the day, I thought about it when there was time. As a medical student and as an intern, I had developed a great respect for anesthesiologists. The day was long gone when all an anesthesiologist did was hold a cotton wad of ether at a patient's nose. Due to some extent to the war, important strides had been made in this field of medicine. New kinds of anesthetics were being used; complicated equipment was being introduced. Anesthesiologists were becoming a vital part of surgery. During an operation, it was the anesthesiologist who gave the surgeons a minute-by-minute report on the patient's condition. I had seen anesthesiologists save lives by their skill, their alert minds, their confidence. The idea began to appeal to me more and more.

That evening I waited until the dinner dishes were done before I told Jo about the development. She listened patiently and lovingly, as she always did whenever I would come up with some unexpected idea.

Then she asked: "Joe, are you giving up your plan of someday having your own gynecology practice?"

"No, I'm not," I said. "But until we see how far this M.S. is going to go, I think we should consider alternative plans."

"And anesthesiology is an alternative?"

"For now. It means a job until we see what happens. If I find out that I like it, I may stay with it. And if I find out in a couple of years that I am able to go into something else, I'm sure that whatever I learn about anesthesiology will be very helpful." We were quiet a few moments. I asked: "What shall we do, Babe?"

She said: "Whatever you say."

I had to take the long view. Any young professional man

41

starting out in business on his own knows he is going to have a slow beginning. Not knowing how far my multiple sclerosis was going to advance or how fast, I had to face the fact that I might not have time to build up a practice that would be big enough and that I could work at long enough to continue to support my family when I could no longer work. In those days, doctors still made house calls. I would have to be mobile enough for that. I would have to be mobile enough to function in an office and in a hospital. If my mobility should rapidly decrease before I was financially secure, I could be in a lot of trouble, probably deep in debt. The prospect of becoming an anesthesiologist therefore offered several distinct advantages. In the first place, I knew there was a demand for anesthesiologists trained in the latest techniques, and I knew I would get excellent training at Mary Immaculate Hospital. Second, there wouldn't be the chore of opening an office and building up a practice, which could be a matter of years. Once certified, I could go right to work and at the going fees. And I wouldn't have to borrow money to buy a lot of expensive equipment—the hospital would provide it.

The next day I went over to Mary Immaculate for the interview. The doctor who interviewed me was a pleasant man, and we chatted amiably for fifteen or twenty minutes about my medical background and my special interests. Then I said: "Doctor, I feel I should tell you that I have multiple sclerosis."

"I know," he said. "What symptoms do you have?"

"Nothing pronounced," I said. "My legs go weak on me once in a while, mostly my right leg."

He nodded. "You'd let us know if there is any further development?"

"Of course."

"All right." He picked up some forms. "You'll get these back to me as soon as you can, please. We want to make a decision next week."

I thanked him and left. The forms went back to him the

same day. About two weeks later, I was notified that the residency had been given to me.

We needed a place to live. Jo and I spent a few days hunting for an apartment, and then my father gave us some good news. My parents' home was actually a two-family unit, and the upstairs apartment had become available. In effect, I was moving back into the house where I had grown up. Meanwhile, I was learning how to be an anesthesiologist. It was fascinating work. I was sure I had made the right decision. Jo and I were very happy.

VI

WHEN I FINISHED MY RESIDENCY at Mary Immaculate in 1948, I was invited to join the staff as Assistant Attending Anesthesiologist, and I accepted. Just about the same time, I also happily accepted the wonderful news that Jo and I had become parents for the second time. It was a boy. We named him Joseph, more after my father than after me.

And also at the same time, I was becoming more aware of my multiple sclerosis—at least, I found myself giving it more thought than I had before. The occasions of weakness in my right leg were becoming more frequent. I started favoring the leg and depended more and more on my left leg, especially when going up or down stairs. My work wasn't affected except on days when we were very busy and I had to move around a lot. During operations I usually sat or stood at the head of the table anyway, so this was no great problem.

Otherwise, things were going well. When our third child and second son, Jeffrey, was born, Jo and I realized that we would have to get a house. We looked around for close to a year and finally found a house in Lynbrook that we liked. It was an English Tudor house with four levels. There was a basement which we finished with a kitchen, laundry room, dining area and a large sitting room for televison and a bar. My dad did the finishing work, and it was a beautiful living area. Stairs led up from the basement to the first floor and more stairs led up to the second floor, where there were three bedrooms. Later on, we had the attic finished with three more large bedrooms. Prior to our moving out of Brooklyn, our second daughter—and fourth child—Jacqueline, was born. After moving into Lynbrook, Jennifer and Judy were born.

For several years, things went along pretty well. Then I began having trouble with all those stairs. We installed hand-rails; and with these and some assistance, I was able to go up and down without too much difficulty. We developed a system. Going up stairs, Jo would stand behind me and lift up one foot a step at a time, and then my sons, Joseph or Jeffrey, whoever was available, would support me from the front. Going down steps, Jo would stand in front and guide my legs one step at a time and the boys would support me to prevent my falling backward. As walking became increasingly difficult, I started using a cane.

One day while returning a post-operative surgical patient to his room—not all hospitals had recovery rooms in those days—I was getting off the elevator when I suddenly found myself sprawled on the floor. I got up quickly, looking around, and I thanked God no one had seen me. But I wondered how long this could go on without it becoming noticeable to others. I continued to have frequent check-ups. The basic problem was that the specialists weren't sure what I had. Although all indications pointed to multiple sclerosis, there were many characteristics of multiple sclerosis that I did not have. There was no doubt, however, that whatever it was was advancing.

We began to entertain less. Occasionally my cousin Russ came to visit and we would reminisce about our youth. The children would gather around and listen to these tales. My son Jeff's favorite story involved an elderly man who ran a general store in our neighborhood when we were boys. There was a pinball machine in the store, and you were supposed to get free candy if you ran up a high enough score. Russ and I became very adept at the machine, I pulling the plunger that sent each ball rolling and Russ standing at the side of the machine using body English to guide the balls into the higher scored holes. But we never got any candy. After a game, we'd call over the owner so that he could see how well we had done, but then the man would apply a little of his own body English to make the tilt sign go on. Then he'd say: "You cheated. You tilted the machine. I don't give you any candy." There was no way we could convince him that he had tilted the machine himself.

One day when this had happened once too often, Russ and I left the store in a rage. In those days, many stores had their milk delivered in bulk in five-gallon metal containers. Customers brought their own containers to buy as much milk as they wanted. This probably wasn't very sanitary, but that's the way it was. That day as we left the store I saw a few containers of milk near the door, and I gave one a kick. It fell over, the milk flooding the whole place.

Russ said: "We'd better get moving."

We started to run. The man, hollering at the top of his lungs, grabbed a stick and came running after us. He was in very good shape for his age. I was in bad shape for mine. This happened while I was recovering from the surgery necessitated by my football injury, so I couldn't run fast. To protect me, Russ lagged behind, just far enough ahead of the old man to avoid being hit by the stick the man was flailing.

We headed for my house. I got there first, ran in and slammed the door behind me. In the door was a window comprised of small, square panels. I watched for Russ, and when he was near enough I opened the door and let him in. Then we slammed the door and locked it. When the old man got to the door, he started banging on it and ringing the bell and hollering; and when he didn't get an answer he started breaking the glass panels with the stick. My mother was upstairs in her sewing room. Hearing the noise, she came downstairs to see what was going on. When she saw the broken glass and the old man outside breaking more panels, my mother went into rage the likes of which I never saw before or after. She opened the door and she and the man went into oral combat in both Italian and English. When they calmed down, the man was insisting on being paid for his milk and my mother was insisting on being paid for the broken window. Finally they compromised. Neither of them would get paid for anything. But that wasn't the end of it for Russ and me. We had to clean up all the broken glass. Then we had to go back to the store and clean up that mess. And we weren't allowed to see each other for a month.

Another exploit Russ enjoyed telling was an experience for which we never got punished because we didn't get caught. In those days, parents didn't give kids allowances. If a kid wanted some money, he had to negotiate for it with his parents in terms of additional chores. But we figured out a way to get around that. Every morning our parents gave us a dime, and we were supposed to use the money for the round trip by elevated train to our high school, the fare then being a nickel. We did this for a while, but then we decided that we were just throwing good money away. We found out that our neighborhood was being serviced every day by a coal-and iceman whose next neighborhood of customers was close to our school. Every morning, our subway dimes in our pockets, we would hunt down the man and ask him for a ride to school, and he always said yes. Our school required boys to wear white shirts and ties, but by the time Russ and I got to school after the ride in the coal truck our shirts weren't white. When our teachers asked us why we had soiled shirts, we would say that our mothers didn't have time to do any laundry, and when our mothers asked us why we had soiled shirts we would say we had been playing baseball or football at school. After school, depending on the weather, we usually walked home. By the end of the week, we each had about thirty or thirty-five cents in our pockets. Outside the school was a street vendor who sold hot dogs and soft drinks, and if you bought two hot dogs you got the drinks free. Every Friday after school Russ and I would go on a spree, stuffing ourselves with the hot dogs and free drinks, this despite the fact that it was Friday and we were supposed to be Catholics who shouldn't eat meat on Friday and also despite the fact that we knew we both had mothers who were excellent cooks and would have wonderful dinners waiting for us when we got home. I guess the fun of it was feeling we were pulling off a fast one on our parents, and we enjoyed the pleasure for a long time. I don't remember whether we even mentioned the Friday meat in confession. Maybe we felt that pulling off a fast one on our parents was a prerogative, not a sin.

Like most boys, we looked forward to cigarettes almost as much as we looked forward to girls. When we were old enough to have a few extra pennies in our pockets, we started buying cigarettes at a neighborhood store where you could buy them one or two at a time. We bought the cheapest brands. We knew that our parents didn't want us to smoke, so we did our smoking outside the neighborhood. I don't think either of us enjoyed it much; but it made us feel manly, and we enjoyed that very much.

During one smoking session, we forgot about the time, then realized that we had to be home in a few minutes. Russ asked: "What do we do about the smell of tobacco on our breath?"

I reached out to a nearby bush and scraped off several leaves. "Chew on these," I said. I don't know how I knew about chlorophyll. We never got sick from smoking, but we both sure got sick from those leaves that time.

Another time when we thought we were in a safe area for smoking, we rounded a corner and ran into our cousin Rose and my Aunt Mary. We tried to bribe them by offering them a puff, feeling they would not tell on us if they tried it, too. We were not successful. This time, Russ and I were not allowed to see each other for two weeks.

With time, I learned that I could still function as long as I trained myself to adjust to the changes that were occurring in me. For example, at one point I noticed that my right hand was growing weaker. I could still use it, but holding a pen or handling medical equipment was becoming difficult. My left hand seemed to be all right, so I knew what I had to do. I spent tedious and endless hours training myself to write with my left hand and to perform with my left hand all the functions I had instinctively performed with my right hand all my life. In effect, I had to train myself to think lefty. With time, I became adept at using my left hand for spinal punctures and spinal anesthesia; and since I still had sufficient strength in my right hand, I was able to give respiratory assistance during inhalation anesthesia.

But then there were still those stairs at home. I had reached the point where I had developed a fear of them. The children were small and not always available, and rather than rely on Jo all the time, I had to schedule my life in a way that made the stairs a last resort in whatever I wanted to do.

What distressed me most was facing the fact that perhaps I might not be able to practice medicine at all. The mere thought was both depressing and terrifying. What would I do with my life? How could I support my family? What kind of a husband would I be?

One night when Jo and I were making love, I had to confess: "I'm sorry, Babe. I don't have enough strength in my arms."

She said: "We'll manage."

And we did.

VII

My mother kept praying for a miracle.

As a Catholic, I could believe miracles were possible.

As a doctor, I wasn't expecting one.

I don't recall that I ever once asked: "Why me?" I had been a doctor long enough to know that people get sick and people have accidents and people are sometimes the victims of being born, and there is no "Why me?" involved. It just happens. I just hoped and prayed that I wouldn't get any worse than I was. I worried, naturally, but not about myself. I worried about Jo and the kids and the payments on the house and car. I wished I could be more helpful around the house and with the children. Now that I could no longer take my morning walks and pick up the day's groceries, the job of running the house fell more and more on Jo. My sons Joseph and Jeffrey were reaching the age where they should have had a father who could go out in the backyard with them and play catch or shoot baskets—things I could not do. I regretted my helplessness, but I wasn't bitter about it. I felt that as long as I was alive I had a lot to live for. And I wanted very much to live.

The children accepted my immobility as uneventfully as though I had merely gone bald. When I needed some help getting around the house, the older children would make themselves available so I could lean on them for balance. Or if

I had difficulty getting up, they would assist me into an upright position. They were not capable of giving me all the physical help I needed, but they were always ready to run and get papers and books for me.

Sometimes Jo had to go out—to shop for food and clothes for the children and other things we needed. This put the children and me on our own for a few hours, and we usually made a party out of it. A popular project was preparing a meal. Almost invariably, we'd make an omelet because this gave us a chance to raid the refrigerator for leftovers. The routine was always the same. Jeanine would crack the eggs into a big bowl and beat them. Then we'd all move in on the refrigerator.

Jackie might say: "Here are some boiled potatoes."

I'd say: "Cut them into cubes, honey, and put them in the eggs."

Joseph would say: "Here's some ham from the other night."

I'd say: "Okay, put in a few slices. Jeff, is there any cheese?"

"Yeah, Daddy. Three kinds."

"Put in a little of each."

Jennifer might say: "How about some onions?"

"Right. Onions. And tomatoes, if there are any."

Judy was too young to be of much help, but she would climb on my lap and watch all the activity.

On and on we would go, until the bowl of eggs was as thick as stew. Then the boys would set the table while the girls did the cooking. It didn't make any difference where anybody sat, and whoever sat next to me just went ahead and fed me when feeding myself started to become increasingly difficult. As the children got older, we experimented with meat sauces for the pasta or gravies for the leftover roast or making croquettes from Sunday's chicken. It was always a lot of fun.

Saturdays were for chores, the girls on the inside, the boys outside, with Jo supervising the girls and I supervising the boys. I knew how eager my sons were to take off with their friends, but they knew I would not let them go until the chores were done. To speed things up, I often tried to draft the friends into pitching in on the work. I'd say: "Why don't a couple of you help Joseph rake up those leaves and put them into the trash bag?" Or: "How about somebody going into the garage and help Jeffrey clean out the car?" With time each batch of new friends learned not to get to our house too early on Saturdays, unless they wanted to do some work.

From time to time there'd come a morning when I just didn't have the strength to get up, so I'd just stay in bed. I could be sure that throughout the day the children would come to me, one by one, to see if I needed anything or just to chat for a few minutes. Jeanine, as the oldest, could always be relied upon to care for the younger children and was always ready with Band-Aids and first-aid treatments. I guess this was the beginning of her nursing career. Jackie acquired her love for art at an early age, and she would come to my room and sit on the bed and sketch as we talked. When she tired of sketching, she would stretch out beside me and we would talk until we were both ready for a nap. Jennifer was always neat and tidy. Her room was always the neatest—she would even fold her dirty clothes. She was solicitous at all times and had a fondness for young children. She eventually became a second mother to James when he came along. Judy acquired her love of animals at an early age; so she would bring her ailing strays to me and I would diagnose their condition and prescribe treatment. Joseph developed a good knack with tools, and he saved me considerable expense. I would tell him what to do and he usually did the job well. He always made sure that the girls would help Jo. Years later, James would bring me his countless gadgets that were always breaking down and, with a little persuasion, I would get Joseph and Jeff to fix them. And, years later, I could look back and see how my children, each in their own ways, made a point of keeping themselves part of my life by keeping me part of theirs. With time I became increasingly dependent upon my children, but they let me know that they were dependent on me, too.

When the children got older and began to date, it was perhaps the Italian in me that made me stricter with the girls than I was with the boys. I wouldn't let one of the girls date a boy who wasn't willing to come into the house first to chat for a few minutes with Jo and me before the two of them took off. I was severely strict about curfews. Any boy who consistently brought one of my daughters home late was blacklisted. And it didn't bother me when one of the girls would come home on time, check in with Jo and me and then, without saying a word, slip out to the front porch to spend a little more time with her date. At least I knew she was within summoning range.

As each of my daughters grew old enough to date, she would take on a habit of her older sisters, a habit that always amused me. Before going out, the girls would present themselves to my son Jeffrey for his opinion of their appearance. I never found out where Jeff acquired the talent, but he had a good eye for such things. If he didn't like the way one of his sisters had done her hair, he told her, showed her how to fix it and often did the fixing himself. He had a good taste for colors. Many times—and without a word of complaint—one of the girls would go back to her room to change something Jeff felt was clashing with something else. My children had their battles, naturally, like all kids, but always the combat was quickly over, and there were no grudges. Although the children all had friends outside the family, these relationships never seemed as close as the relationships within the family. Maybe it was my dependence upon the children and their sense of responsibility toward me that created a stronger interdependence among them. I know that, these days, the easiest way to keep my youngest son James around the house for a few minutes is to have my oldest son Joseph come and spend a few days with us. When they are within sight of each other, Joseph and James are inseparable. But all of our children are like that to some degree, and that's the way Jo and I like it.

Jo and I rarely discussed my condition. Our husband and wife talks were the same as the talks of other husbands and wives—the children, bills, upkeep of the house and car, relatives and friends who seemed to have worse problems than we did. We had to be selective in our vacation plans because, year after year, there was less that I could do. On the mornings when I didn't have enough strength to dress myself, Jo would move in and help without being asked or asking. Some nights I didn't have the energy to write up the progress reports on my cases at the hospital. Sensing this, Jo would pick up a pad and a pencil and say: "Joe, dictate the reports to me. I want to keep up on my shorthand." Then she'd type up the reports, just as she did with my notes while I was in college and medical school.

During our first few years of marriage, Jo and I were kept busy, what with my work at the hospital and emergency calls from other hospitals in need of an anesthesiologist. Jo, of course, had the children. However, we still had a fairly active social life. Many times we entertained at home or visited friends. Frequently there were social events involving the hospital—banquets, dances. When the children began to come and we needed a babysitter, my mother was always available. Gradually things slowed down. First, the dancing stopped. Then friends started decreasing their visits and their invitations. At first I wondered if my increasing paralysis was becoming an embarrassment to them, but then I realized what was wrong. It was becoming difficult for them to reciprocate. Most of them lived in houses that had a lot of stairs or maybe no easily accessible bathroom on the first floor. The subject was a bit too sensitive to bring up, so Jo and I just announced that because of my increased difficulty in walking we wouldn't be going out much but that our friends would always be welcomed at our home at any time.

My sister Lucretia, her husband and their children usually came over on Fridays for dinner and talk and cards. From time to time they would suggest that they arrive after dinner so that Jo wouldn't go through the trouble of preparing a big dinner, but Jo wouldn't hear of it. I never learned how she did it, but Jo could always prepare a feast for twelve, spending hardly any time in the kitchen at all.

Our most frequent visitors were my parents. My mother was crazy about the kids and they were crazy about her. My mother was the only person who invariably questioned me about my condition. She never really settled down for a visit until I had given her a detailed medical report on how things were going for me at the moment.

Then she'd say: "Joe, I'm still praying."

"Thanks, Ma."

"And, Joe, believe me, when God closes one door He always opens another."

"I know, Ma. I just hope God hasn't closed any doors on me yet."

And then one day the door closed with a bang.

One wintry morning in 1953, I left the house early so I could arrive at the hospital in plenty of time to set up for an operation. The streets were very icy, so I drove slowly and carefully. I reached the intersection where I always made a left turn and I stopped for the traffic. I saw a car approaching the same intersection to my left. Because of the ice, I decided to let the driver proceed before making the turn. I had the right of way, and the driver evidently thought I was going to take it. He jammed on his brakes. I saw the car go into a spin, then into a slide, heading straight for me. There wasn't time for me to back up or move ahead. I braced myself for the crash.

The car struck me with such force that my door sprang open and I fell out of the car. My arms shot out and protected the upper part of my body but the rest of me hit the pavement like dead weight. People came running.

Some asked: "Are you all right?"

"I think so."

"Can you get up?"

"No. I'm partially paralyzed."

"Oh my God."

"Not from this. Multiple sclerosis."

"What can I do for you?"

"Please call an ambulance."

X rays showed that I hadn't broken any bones. I could see for myself that my body was covered with bruises. And I was full of aches and pains all over. I had someone call Jo, and she came to the hospital right away. After I convinced her that I was all right, I asked her about the car, and she said it was a wreck and had been picked up by a local garage. As a safeguard, I spent the night in the hospital, and in the morning I went home. I decided to take a few days off.

Although I received no serious injuries from the accident, I knew something had happened to me. I sensed it more than felt it, the way you can sense that someone is staring at you. Something had changed inside me. I did not know what it was but I was very much aware of it.

Before long, I perceived that the tempo of the multiple sclerosis had apparently increased. I was always tired. I had no energy for anything, no interest in anything. At times I could hardly speak above a whisper.

Jo noticed it. She asked: "Why don't you see a doctor?"

I said: "I am a doctor."

"Do you know what's wrong with you?"

"I'm not sure. Maybe the M.S. has flared up."

"Why don't you get a second opinion?"

I knew that I should, but I was afraid of a second opinion. I had lived with multiple sclerosis for ten years. The deterioration had been steadfast but slow. Now, since the accident, it seemed to be galloping, and I realized I might not have much longer to be functional. The same fear that kept me from the doctors finally drove me to them. If I was going to become completely dependent, I wanted to know how much time I had left—there was so much to be done.

I made the rounds of the specialists who had been giving me checkups for years. Most of them agreed that the M.S. was on a rampage, and none of them wanted to make any prognosis.

But one specialist said: "Joe, I've never really been convinced that you have M.S."

"I know," I said. "A couple of other men have said that. Well, if I don't have M.S., what do I have?"

"Could be a tumor."

"Where?"

"There," he said, and he touched the back of my neck. He said: "I've run into this a few times in the past four or five years. The tumor creates all the symptoms of multiple sclerosis—gradual paralysis until it is complete."

"Multiple sclerosis can lie dormant for years," I pointed out.

"That's true," he said, "but the tumor won't."

"What are my chances if I have surgery?"

"If it's a tumor, you should be back on your feet in a few weeks and have some recovery from your present disability."

"And if it isn't a tumor?"

"You may be in a wheelchair for the rest of your life."

"There's no way to tell in advance?"

"No. X ray doesn't pick it up. We have to go in there and look."

I thought about it. "I think I'd better talk this over with my wife," I said.

Jo and I had a long talk about it. In a way, I had little choice. If I had multiple sclerosis and it was advancing as fast as it seemed to be, I had no future except the wheelchair and always the threat of total dependence. If I had no tumor, the future would be just about the same. But if I had a tumor and it was removed, I would be a new man, the man I used to be.

We decided to go ahead with the operation because we both knew I would never have peace within me if I did not elect to have surgery performed.

The night before the operation, Jo had dinner with me in my room at the hospital. I felt so optimistic. I was in such high spirits. I said: "Just think Babe, if this works we can go dancing again."

"That would be wonderful," she said. "But whatever happens, it will be God's will."

Next morning, as I was wheeled on a table into the operating room, my only thought was: "It's up to you, God. I'll accept whatever you decide. But if you've closed the door already, please don't forget about the other one."

VIII

I COULD FEEL MYSELF coming out of the anesthetic.

My eyes closed, I waited for the pain. There was no pain.

I tried to wiggle my toes, but I could not be sure whether they were wiggling or not.

I opened my eyes. Jo was standing at the side of the bed, holding my hand. I thought I felt her hand in mine.

I said: "Is it a boy or a girl?"

She said: "Which would you like?"

I said: "I'd like a benign tumor."

She looked at me a long time, then said: "There was no tumor, hon. They didn't find anything."

Tears streamed down the side of my face. At that moment, my hopes for a productive future ended. I could not hold back the tears. And I said: "Let's go home, Babe."

"In a few days."

I had taken the gamble and I had lost.

If I had let the multiple sclerosis proceed on its own, perhaps I wouldn't have become a paraplegic so suddenly. And I knew I hadn't reached the end of the line. The rest of me would go, too, maybe not so suddenly but inevitably. I felt the walls closing in on me. My life was over.

When I got home I discovered that Jo had converted the dining room into a bedroom for me, complete with a hospital bed. This, I thought, is the way it's going to be for me from now on. Helpless. Useless.

The children were still too young to understand what had happened to me. They kept coming into the room with their games and toys and problems. I said to Jo: "Listen, keep the kids away from me, will you? I'm not ready for them."

"They are ready for you," she said, "and I don't want them to feel that they don't have a father."

"They don't."

"Then you'll have to tell them that."

I didn't want to see anybody. The first visit of my parents was a torment for me. My mother tried to be brave, but there were tears in her eyes, and she kept looking at me as though I was in my coffin. My father kept saying: "Don't worry about a thing, don't worry about a thing."

I didn't worry about a thing. I knew worrying wouldn't do any good. I just wondered how I was going to survive watching my whole life go down the drain. Maybe it was a good thing that Jo kept up on her shorthand. Most likely, she would have to go out and get a job to support the family. My earning days were certainly over.

I had been home a couple of weeks, still spending most of my time in bed, when one afternoon Jo said to me: "Honey, I want you to get dressed and have dinner with the family this evening."

I knew that the family was taking meals in the kitchen or down in the family room. I said: "That's too much trouble."

"Not for us," she said. "Why should it be for you?"

I grasped for excuses. "I can't get down to the family room in a wheelchair."

"You don't have to," Jo said. "We'll eat in the living room. I'll make a big buffet and it'll be like a picnic. Come on, get dressed. The children would love seeing you sitting up when they come home from school."

"That's too much trouble."

"It isn't any trouble at all," she said firmly.

She pulled back the sheets on my bed and started removing my pajamas. I was lifeless from the waist down and, being a large man, a lot of dead weight.

I said: "You're in no shape to do this."

She said: "Then I'd better get in shape if I'm going to do this for the rest of my life."

She went upstairs and got some casual clothes from my closet in our bedroom. Dressing me required real effort, especially lifting me to put on the underwear and the pants. When I was finally dressed, Jo took hold of my ankles and brought my body around so that my feet touched the floor. I still had enough strength in my arms to make myself sit up. Jo brought close to the bed the wheelchair we had rented following my discharge from the hospital. Then she put my right arm around her shoulders, and she said: "Okay, honey, let's dance." Bracing me, she swung me around and I settled into the wheelchair. She adjusted my feet on the footrest, and then she pushed me into the living room. "Now, then," she said, "remember this place?"

I had almost forgotten it, not because I hadn't seen it for a few weeks but because I was beginning to think that I never would see it again. The room was immaculate, as it usually was. Jo had placed flowers everywhere, knowing how much I liked flowers.

She asked: "Want to watch some television?"

"No. Not now."

"Want to read the paper? You haven't looked at a paper for a long time."

"No. I heard the news on the radio."

"You're just going to sit there?"

"What else can I do? I can't get back to bed on my own."

"Then how about some juice?"

"All right. I am a bit thirsty."

"The children will be home in a few minutes. You know how excited they'll be, especially when they see you sitting up."

"I guess."

Jo went out to the kitchen to get the juice for us, and she was just coming with them when the front door burst open and in rushed our children who were old enough to go to school. They rushed right past me, either out to the kitchen to get something to eat or up to their rooms to change.

I asked Jo: "Do you think they saw me?"

"I don't know," she said. "Give them a few minutes."

A few minutes was all it took. Back the kids came in the same roar that had brought them into the house. They chattered with me about things that had happened at school that day, they showed me their good marks on tests, the television set went on accompanied by a battle over which channel to watch. Heavy footsteps kept racing up and down the stairs. And there was an endless parade to the kitchen for something to eat.

Ordinarily, I did not witness this after-school invasion, work keeping me out of the house until dinnertime, by then most of the steam out of the kids. And after my operation, Jo had ordered the children to be quiet around the house. I suppose that seeing me sitting up in my wheelchair made the kids think that whatever was wrong with me was over now and they returned to normal.

I looked at Jo. "Is it always like this?"

"Every single day."

"How do you put up with it?"

"I guess you can put up with anything once you face the fact that you must."

"I guess so."

Jo brought a tray of snacks and fruit that was immediately attacked by the children. After their stormy return from school, I expected the chaos to continue, but gradually peace was restored. None of the kids sat still very long, making frequent trips to the snacks, but the volume was turned down, and I started feeling glad that Jo had made me get up. I was sitting too far from the snacks to help myself, but from time to time one of the children would bring the tray to me. From time to time one of them would serve the others. And from time to time one of the girls would go out to the kitchen to help Jo. That such orderliness could gradually come out of the initial bedlam indicated to me that the children had gone through this before, probably every day, and I realized that there had to be some mastermind who could train these six strong-willed individuals to function as a team. It could only be Jo. I saw further proof of this as dinner approached.

Jo came into the room and announced: "All right, dinner is just about ready. I'm going to need some help. Turn off the television set somebody." The television set went off. Jo said: "Dinner is going to be buffet style in here. Joseph, why don't you put up a couple of card tables side by side? Use the green tablecloth that's in the linen closet. Jeanine, I'll need you in the kitchen for a minute. Jeff, you can put out the silverware, and we'll need about a dozen serving spoons. The rest of you can start carrying things in."

It was like watching an assembly line go into action. In a couple of minutes the living room was transformed into a banquet hall, the card tables loaded with a dozen different kinds of food. I wondered when Jo found time to prepare it all. Ordinarily I didn't see this side of dinner. Usually the table was set and the food ready when I came in from work. So I had witnessed something few husbands see: the management side of being a wife and mother.

The kids didn't wait to be told to dig in. At one point, Joseph said: "Dad, do you want me to fix you a plate?"

Before I could answer, Jo said: "Just help yourself, Joseph. And if Dad needs help, I'll help him."

I waited until the kids had dug big holes in the mountains of food, then wheeled myself to the tables and fixed a plate. Although everybody was eating, there was still a lot of conversation in the room. The children seemed to feel that everything that happened to them and to each other was important. Everybody had something to say, and everybody else had questions and comments. Ordinarily I had too much on my own mind to pay much attention to the dinner chatter, except when one of the kids got a little rowdy. This time, listening because there was nothing else for me to do, I was beginning to see how interesting my children were. Jo evidently already knew this. She was right in there on the conversations no matter which turns they took.

After dinner, the banquet hall became the living room again with the same assembly-line precision. Then the television set went on, followed by a brief skirmish over what we would watch. Jeanine suggested a vote, and a Western won. After it, Jo said: "Isn't it homework time now?" There were groans from the older kids who were in school, but they got up reluctantly and went to their rooms and their books.

Around nine, I said: "Jo, I'm getting tired. Help me back to bed, will you?"

"Sure," she said. "Maybe we overdid it for the first day."

"No," I said. "I enjoyed it."

"So did I. Tomorrow if the weather is nice, let's have the picnic out in the garden."

I said: "All right."

After that, I usually got up for dinner, and gradually I started getting up earlier and staying up later. I realized that if we were to continue using the living room as a dining room, I would either have to move upstairs or build an addition to the house. Jo and I decided that we could convert our garage into a bedroom and bath without too much difficulty. We called in contractors, and before we knew it we were also making plans to build a new garage on the other side of the house which we could drive into and add a ramp for easy accessibility into the house.

We lived this way for a while, but we had a problem. Jo had to sleep upstairs to be near the children and I slept alone downstairs. Often during the night I had to call Jo through an intercom, and this meant her going up and down stairs in the middle of the night. It was becoming more and more difficult for her since she was pregnant.

One day while I was wondering what to do about the stairs, Jo said: "Guess what I thought of today, honey?"

"I can't," I said. "Tell me."

She said: "Why don't we have an elevator installed here in the house?"

"An elevator?"

"Yes. You can still use the wheelchair and go anywhere you want whenever you want."

"Can that be done in this house?"

"I don't know," she said. "I just thought of it today. I'll check it out."

She checked it out and learned that the idea was feasible. It was also expensive. For weeks the house was torn apart as carpenters made the holes in the floors and engineers installed the elevator equipment. I didn't like the thing from the start. I never felt safe in it. It was merely a waist-high cage held in place by metal poles and moved by cables. The cage had a gate, and there were gates at each floor. I still had the use of my arms, so usually I could manage on my own. But I was worried about the children. The older ones were very active, and I didn't want any of them to fall down the shaft. Actually it was Jo who fell down the shaft. Intent on her housework one day, she was unaware that a gate had somehow become open. She backed into the shaft and then found herself sprawled on the floor down in the basement. She was badly shaken up and somewhat bruised but, fortunately, not seriously injured. After that, we had the gates fixed so that the children could not open them and they could not open by themselves.

The elevator kept giving us trouble. One day I was going up in the elevator when a cable broke and the car went into a deep tilt, practically putting me on my back. There was no one in the house who could help me except Jo, and there was nothing she could do. I had to hang there on my back in midair for two hours until the repairmen arrived and replaced the cable and uprighted the car. Many times, Joseph and Jeffrey had to handcrank the elevator when the cable came off the pulley. Although the elevator was used for many years, I always approached it with great trepidation.

I had nothing to do and I was bored. I could not get myself out of the dumps. Jo tried to keep me busy with talk and reading and television. I became quite an expert at Scrabble during this time. But no matter what was going on, a part of me always ached with despair. I could not keep my bleak future out of my mind. I did not become better, but I was feeling hopeless—and that is worse.

One morning, Jo said to me: "You must be getting stir-crazy. Let's go for a drive."

"Why go for a drive?" I asked.

"So you can get out of the house," she said, "and get some fresh air and a change of scenery. It'll be good for you, Joe."

I didn't want to go, but I could see that Jo had her heart set on it. After helping me in and out of bed so often, she had no trouble getting me into the car. We drove around town for a while and then headed out into the country. When you are driving you don't have much opportunity to enjoy the scenery. With Jo driving, I found myself enjoying the scenery. I knew this part of Long Island like I knew the palm of my hand, and yet I felt I was seeing many things for the first time.

After a couple of hours, Jo said: "There's a wonderful farmers' market up ahead."

"Yes, I know."

"Let's go in and browse around."

"Honey, I don't want to go into the market in a wheelchair. You go in and browse if you want to. I'll wait in the car."

"It's no fun to browse alone. Besides, I want you to pick out what you want for dinner tonight. I'm tired of trying to think up menus."

I knew what Jo was trying to do and I did not want to disappoint her. I never spoke to Jo about my low spirits but I was sure she was aware of them. So we went in and browsed. I remembered the old days when I would buy the day's groceries on my early morning walks. Well, that would never happen again. In a few minutes, I became so fascinated by the amazing amounts of food piled up all over the market that I felt like a kid turned loose in a toy factory. We were there over an hour and practically bought out the place.

66

A week or so later, I was in the living room reading the paper one morning when the phone rang and Jo took the call in the kitchen. I couldn't hear what she was saying, but then she came to me and said: "That was Sam. He and the other fellows and their wives want to take us out to dinner Friday night."

"In a restaurant?"

"Yes. Where else?"

"I can't eat in a restaurant in this wheelchair."

"Oh, I'm sure it's been done before."

"I'm not going to try it. Call Sam back and say we can't make it."

"I'm not going to lie. We can make it. Anyway, I've already accepted."

"Then I'll call him back."

"Go ahead. He'll be very disappointed. It's St. Joseph's Day. And my birthday."

So I had to go. At the end of the meal, the headwaiter brought a small birthday cake with one lighted candle on it and the whole place sang "Happy Birthday" to Jo. Her eyes glistened with joy, and that was enough for me to forget any inconvenience of getting into the restaurant and making my way to the table and maybe blocking the traffic for a few moments. It wasn't as bad as I had figured.

There was little money coming in. We had enough in our savings to carry us for four or five months, plus a few small investments, and that was about it. A friend who was a lawyer suggested that since I had developed multiple sclerosis while I was in the Army the Veterans Administration might regard my disability as being service-incurred and grant me a pension. I didn't think so, but he went ahead and checked it out anyway. I was granted a small pension, and this certainly was a tremendous help but still not enough to support our large family.

One day I got a letter from one of the doctors at the hospital saying that he and a few other doctors wanted to take up a collection for me. This was a thoughtful gesture, I suppose, and I appreciated it; but it was also charity, and I knew I could never accept the money. I wrote back thanks but no thanks—I'd manage somehow.

The chief anesthesiologist at Mary Immaculate was Dr. Grace Frank, who taught me everything I ever learned about anesthesiology. We were a group of four anesthesiologists at the hospital. As with all groups, we shared our income. We never had a formal contract. We were a very closely knit group, working together, sharing cases and night calls. Dr. Frank was also a very dear friend and a generous person. When it became known that I could never return to anesthesiology, she very quietly sent me a small check each month. This continued for two years. It was this more than anything else that kept the family off welfare.

Jo kept up her tricks for getting me out of the house two or three times a week. One day we were driving somewhere and I glanced at her protruding abdomen. I said: "You're just about due, aren't you, Babe?"

"Any day now," she said.

But days passed and nothing happened. Then weeks passed. A month. Several times I wakened to see Jo sitting in a chair praying. When I asked her what was wrong, she said nothing. Finally she admitted that she wasn't feeling much activity, although her doctor said he could still hear the fetal heart.

Then one night Jo went into labor. She packed a bag and my sister's husband John Rowley drove her to the hospital. My mother moved into the house to take care of the kids and me. I kept calling the labor room to see how Jo was. Things seemed to be going normally, though unusually slowly. I was getting concerned.

The call came the second evening. My mother took it. I heard her say: "Hello? Yes. Yes, Doctor, he's right here." She looked at me. "Joe, it's the obstetrician."

I knew the man well. I took the phone eagerly. "Hi. Is it a boy or a girl?"

"It was twins, Joe."

"That's wonderful. How's Jo?"

"She's all right. Joe—"

His voice had a warning. "Yes?"

"The babies were stillbirths."

"Oh my God."

"I'm sorry, Joe. There was nothing we could do."

"I understand. Does Jo know?"

"Yes."

"How is she taking it?"

"She seems to be all right, but I'm sure she's broken-hearted."

"I'm sure she is."

"I'm sorry, Joe."

"Thanks." I hung up. I said: "I'm going to the hospital."

My mother said: "You're going where?"

"To the hospital. I've got to be with Jo."

"What's the matter? Is something wrong?"

"Yes. Jo had twins. They were born dead."

"My God." She made the sign of the cross on herself.

"I've got to go to her. I've got to be with Jo."

"How are you going to get there?"

"In my car." I was already heading for the door.

"Joe, don't drive," my mother said. "You haven't driven since the operation. It could be dangerous."

"I don't care. Jo shouldn't be alone."

"Let me call John. He'll drive you."

"I can't wait for John."

"Then let me call a cab."

"I can't wait for a cab, either."

"Joe, don't do this."

"I have to. I want to be with Jo."

Somehow I got out of the house. Somehow I got into the car and pulled in the wheelchair after me. Somehow I got the car started and drove to the hospital. Somehow I got the wheelchair and me out of the car and into the hospital. Somehow I got to Jo's room. I still don't remember a minute of the whole trip.

When I entered Jo's room, she seemed to be asleep. She looked exhausted, so small. Then she heard me and looked at me. She was so amazed to see me that she sat up and said: "Joe!" She almost screamed it.

I wheeled myself to the bed and took Jo into my arms. We were both crying. I don't know how long we remained that way, but after a while we regained our composure and I helped her lie down. We dried our eyes.

She asked: "How did you get here?"

"I drove."

"You drove yourself?" She couldn't believe it.

"Yes."

"Oh, Joe, you shouldn't have done that. It was too dangerous."

"I didn't care. I wanted to be with you."

"I'm glad you are."

Then we talked about the twins, about how much we would have loved them, what fun it would have been to raise them. We talked about our other children. We talked about us.

I said: "Babe, I'm going to get a job. I don't know how or where I'll find it, but I'm going to get a job."

"I know you will."

"I want to come back to the human race."

"You never left it."

On that, my brother-in-law John came barging into the room, his face all fear and anger. He barked at me: "Are you crazy, driving here by yourself? Your mother's a nervous wreck. I'll call her and let her know you made it. God, you lunatic, somebody up there must be looking after you."

When he came back, he was calm, and the three of us chatted until it was time to go. John drove me in my car, a friend of his following in his car.

Along the way, I said: "John, I'm going to get myself a job."

"I'm sure you will," he said. "After this, nothing will keep you home now."

But finding a job turned out to be much more difficult than I expected.

After Jo came home from the hospital and rested a few

70

days, we made a list of everybody I knew in medicine who was in a position to give me a job if I qualified. The most promising fields were psychiatry, X ray and teaching. Then I either called or wrote the people I knew and set up interviews. Jo drove me around. One appointment after another led to nothing. Either I didn't qualify or there were no openings or there was no opening for a man in my condition.

One doctor told me: "Joe, if I were you I'd start learning how to repair watches." If I could have stood up to do it, I would have hit him. Jo was furious.

One day I had an interview with the head of a psychiatric hospital, and he said: "I wouldn't think of putting a disabled doctor on my staff."

"Why not?" I asked.

He said: "Because you would be unable to defend yourself if a patient became violent."

He probably had a point, but I knew too that many disabled people could have psychiatric problems, and I was hoping to work with them.

Later, I was having an interview with a doctor who had an important administrative position in a large hospital in Manhattan, and he asked: "Joe, have you thought about rehabilitation?"

I was surprised. "For me? I'm too late for that."

"Not as therapy for you," he said. "As a job."

"Rehabilitation medicine?"

"Yes. Have you thought about it?"

"No. It never occurred to me."

"Well, what do you think of it now?"

"I'm not sure. I know so little about it."

"Do you know Howard Rusk?"

"I know who he is."

"He's just about the best man we have around in rehab medicine."

"I know."

"Howard and I are pretty good friends. Why don't I call him and set up an appointment for you with him in a few days? It might help you make up your mind."

"I'd be grateful."

I liked Dr. Howard A. Rusk on sight. He was a tall, handsome man, with a strong personality and a gentle manner. We had the meeting in his office at the Institute of Rehabilitation Medicine, which he had founded and now headed as part of the New York University–Bellevue Medical Center. He was also a no-nonsense man. After questioning me for ten or fifteen minutes about my background and my multiple sclerosis, he asked: "When did you become interested in rehabilitation medicine?"

I said: "To tell you the truth, Doctor, I never even thought about it until a few days ago. I've had time to do some reading, and I think it's a fascinating field of medicine."

"Would you be interested in going into it?"

"Very much, if I could find a residency for it."

He thought about it, then said: "Well, if you don't believe in the product you're selling, you shouldn't be selling it. We're always telling people to hire the handicapped. We've done it ourselves in the past, and I don't see why you should be an exception. It will require you to take a three-year fellowship here at the institute. Would you be willing to return to school for three more years?"

"In a flash."

"All right," he said. "I'll submit your credentials to the board and I'll sponsor you. I'm supposed to be the boss around here, so there shouldn't be any problems."

"I can't thank you enough."

"Don't bother," he said. "There's one more thing. We give no quarter to anybody around here, no matter what shape he's in."

"I wouldn't want any," I said.

"Very well. I'll be in touch with you in a few days."

Going home, I felt like singing, something I have never done well. I was so happy, and I could see that Jo was too. I was going back to medicine. I was going to practice again.

I beamed at her and said: "Babe, I think God has just opened the other door."

72

IX

I LOVED IT.

I never worked harder in my life, before or since, but I loved it.

There was so much that I had to learn, even more that I had to relearn. Having been in anesthesia for so long, much of the knowledge I had acquired in medical school had moved to the back of my mind, and now I had to bring it up front again. The only way to do that was to return to my books. I had to learn again everything I had been taught about orthopedics, neurology and internal medicine. I had already watched a lot of surgical pathology, and this was a great help. Most of the other residents at the institute were younger men, fresh out of medical school, so the work came easier for them. For me, a senior citizen of thirty-five, the residency meant long hours at home every evening over my books. My kids couldn't figure out how come I had more homework than they did.

For the first couple of weeks, Jo drove me to work in the morning and picked me up in the afternoon, and my mother would stay with the children during these trips. But I soon realized that this would not work and that I would have to become self-dependent and drive by myself. I made arrangements to have hand controls installed in my car. We drove into Long Island City, where the controls were installed.

After the mechanic finished, he demonstrated the controls and then had me drive the car around the block—just once. And that was all the instruction I received.

I took to the controls rather easily, but my impulse to use my feet rather than my hands was hard to overcome. Gradually I regained my confidence in my driving and I made the trips alone. Later on, a fellow resident, Dr. Ewing, a former mechanical engineer, put together an electrical device by which he could easily bring his own wheelchair into his car and out of it without any help from anyone else. I tested it, and it worked so well I had it installed in my car.

Soon after starting the residency, I was assigned for basic training in chronic care to the Goldwater Memorial Hospital on what was then Welfare Island, and is now Roosevelt Island, in the East River. I had to be there at eight o'clock in the morning to take rounds and, because I always drove slowly and carefully, this meant leaving the house at six. To get to the island, I had to go onto the Fifty-ninth Street bridge where there was an elevator that lowered cars down to the island. This part of the trip always terrified me. I was glad when the city built a small bridge from Queens to the island and I no longer had to use that elevator.

Two mornings a week, I had to go to the institute for lectures. On these mornings, I entered Manhattan via the Triborough Bridge, a toll bridge. The toll was twenty-five cents. I usually kept loose change on top of the dashboard. When I saw myself approaching the toll booths, I would put the quarter between my teeth and start slowing down the car. Nearer, I would touch the button that lowered the car window and take the coin out of my mouth so that the toll taker wouldn't see where they came from. Then I'd slow down the car as much as I could without stalling, pass slowly through the toll and drop the coin into the collector's hand. After that, it was an easy trip for me down the FDR Drive, which had no stoplights, to the Thirty-fourth Street exit, a block from the institute. On the mornings when I saw I didn't have the quarter handy I'd enter the city via the Fifty-ninth Street bridge, which didn't have a toll, but this meant very heavy traffic, mostly trucks, and then the trip southward on Second Avenue with traffic lights at every corner and big trucks usually double- or triple-parked.

One morning as I was going in on the Triborough Bridge, my timing must have been off. As I reached out to give the toll taker the coin, I missed his hand and the coin fell to the ground. I stopped the car.

The man said: "Get out and pick it up."

I said: "I can't get out."

"You can't get out?"

"No, I can't."

"Why not?"

"I'm paralyzed."

"You're what?"

"I'm paralyzed. Can't you see the wheelchair in my car?"

Frowning, he got out of the booth to pick up the coin, and he muttered: "Then why are you driving?"

"Because I can't walk," I said, and I drove on. After that, I avoided that man's booth.

The institute had been designed with the handicapped in mind, so I had no problems parking and getting in and out of the building. Inside, when I had a short trip, I'd propel myself along with my hands; on longer trips, there was always somebody to push me. At Goldwater, however, I did have some problems. The hospital was old; the parking area was too small, and part of it was on a slant. Several times I came close to hitting a parked car as I tried to maneuver myself into a vacant space. I tried to park as close to the building as I could so that I wouldn't have too long a trip from my car across the exposed area, so arctic in winter, the wind so strong I wondered when I would get blown into the river, and sometimes I had to sit outdoors until someone saw me or heard me and would help me get inside.

Even so, I enjoyed Goldwater, and I knew I was receiving important training under Dr. Michael Dascho. The hospital had an excellent polio unit, one of the last polio units in the country now that the disease was no longer so rampant. After almost a year at Goldwater, I was assigned to Bellevue, practically next door to the institute, and I continued a day or so a week at the institute. I discovered that Dr. Rusk was a man of his word. Three other residents were also doctors in wheelchairs. We called ourselves the Wheelchair Brigade. They were polio victims, and their disabilities had gone as far as they would go. I still had no idea how far mine was going to go.

Aware of this, I knew that the training during my residency would have to be different from that of the other men. A physical examination required touching the patient; and I knew that the day might come when I would not be able to use my hands and that, if somebody else put my hands on a patient, I wouldn't be able to feel too well anyway. So I had to add something on my own. As long as I could touch and feel, I also looked. With time I could perceive with my eyes many things I could have perceived by touch and feel. I also learned to question a patient far more extensively than the usual physical examination encompassed, and in this way I learned a great deal more about a patient's condition and progress and acquired a better judgment for diagnosis and prescription of therapy. I decided I'd better develop this ability while I had the chance.

I was fortunate that during my training I had a fellow resident from Turkey who happened to have trouble learning the English language. He had been assigned to me since I was chief resident. This gave me the opportunity to have a fellow resident be my constant companion during physical examinations. Ali Fernegraglu and I spent many hours together, I teaching him the English language and he concurring with me as to what I perceived through sight and he by feel. This combination proved invaluable to both of us. To this day we communicate with each other despite the fact that he is in Turkey and it is twenty years since we last saw each other. We always end our letters with the hope that someday we will get together again.

I spent the last six months of my residency at the institute. The days were long and full and fascinating. Mornings began with rounds, followed by examination and treatment of out-patients and new patients, then lectures on all aspects of our work. Most of the residents were from somewhere else and, if they had their wives with them, lived in apartments in Manhattan or, if in town alone, stayed with friends. I was one of the few who commuted daily. Like all the residents, I had to take my turn at night duty. Not many emergency cases were brought in, but occasionally an inpatient would have difficulty during the night and the nurse on duty would call the resident's room. On my duty nights I didn't undress because I didn't want to lose any time if there was a patient who needed me in a hurry. One night I was in too much of a hurry myself. I got a call. And as I swung myself from the bed to my wheelchair I was a bit off balance. The chair slipped from my grasp and I landed on the floor. I tried to get up but I couldn't, so I lay there hollering for help for twenty minutes until an orderly, sent to find out what was keeping me, found me on the floor and helped me into my chair.

The residency also turned out to be a financial lifesaver for me. It paid about twenty-five hundred a year—not much, but this plus the V.A. pension, my disability insurance and legal award of several thousand because of the car accident meant my family was able to make ends meet. Just.

About a month before my residency ended, Dr. Rusk sent for me. He told me that the nearby Beth Israel Hospital was thinking about enlarging its small physical medicine unit. He said: "They've asked me to recommend somebody to super-vise the expansion and then run the place. Are you inter-ested?"

"Yes, I am," I said, "but I'm not sure I'm ready for a job that big just yet."

"I think you are. Otherwise I wouldn't have talked to them about you already."

"Do they know I'm in a wheelchair?"

"Yes. Do you want me to set up an appointment?"

"Yes. Thank you."

I got the job. Starting a new medical career at such a high level scared me a bit. I was determined to do a good job, not just because I wouldn't have considered doing anything less but because I wanted to justify Dr. Rusk's faith in me.

The people at Beth Israel were wonderful. I was given a free hand in designing a larger unit, in supervising the installation and in building up the staff. Beth Israel had decided to enlarge its facility because it was receiving more and more patients who were survivors of the Nazi prison camps and had incurred their disabilities there. Many of them were older and frail. That they had survived at all was a miracle. Every time I saw the prison number tattooed on a patient's arm, I winced. When I thought of all the pain and suffering people endured because of disease and accidents in day-to-day life, I wondered why some people have to inflict even greater pain and suffering to the point of brutality merely out of prejudice. I grew to love my Beth Israel patients. They called me "Dr. Yussef."

Two or three times a week I would go over to the institute to put in the time to complete my residency. When it was completed, I faced my board examinations, both oral and written, which I had to pass to be certified as a specialist in rehabilitation medicine. The orals were held in New York, and I had no trouble with them. For some reason, the written exam was held in Peoria, Illinois.

By this time, I had developed spasticity, and I was expecting it. Paralyzed people often develop spasticity in the affected extremities. People with multiple sclerosis usually do. A spasm can be set off when the person is touched or moved —or just startled—improperly and unexpectedly. Mild spasms can be brief and end by themselves; severe spasms, as in my case, can make my legs jut out stiff as boards, shaking fiercely, and to end the spasm some knowledgeable person has to twist my ankles back and forth slightly and gently, like turning off a vibrator. There is no pain in a spasm but it can be very upsetting, and it can terrify anybody who doesn't know what's going on. Jo has always made jokes about my spasms. Sometimes when a bad one hit me, she would look at me naïvely and ask: "Joe, you want to dance?" And then she would turn off the vibrator.

On the trip to Peoria, Jo and I had no problems at LaGuardia or O'Hare airports because both terminals had ramps that made getting on and off the big planes in my wheelchair as easy as crossing a threshold. On planes, I always had to have the aisle seat in the first row of first class. When I had the strength for it, I could transfer myself from the wheelchair to the seat and back again. Later I had to have help. I was usually the first person on the plane and the last to get off.

On this trip, when we got to Chicago we discovered that the flight to Peoria would be on a smaller airline in a small plane that was boarded via a flight of stairs at the rear. I knew I was in trouble. When we got to the plane, two attendants were waiting there with a regular wooden chair and I transferred myself to it.

I said: "Now, turn me around and carry me up backwards."

Either they didn't hear me or they thought they knew better. One attendant got behind the chair, the other took hold of the front legs, and they picked me up and headed for the stairs.

I kept saying: "Turn me around! Turn me around!"

And Jo kept saying: "Backwards! Backwards!"

On they went to the stairs, and up. The chair went into a sharp tilt, and I was practically standing on my head. A severe spasm hit me. My back went stiff and my legs shot out and I almost kicked the front man in the groin. He probably thought I was having a fit. His expression was sheer terror.

Jo needed a few minutes to turn off the vibrator so I could get into the seat. When everything was finally calm, Jo said: "I'll bet you're one passenger this airline will never forget."

At Peoria, two other attendants were waiting for us. They followed instructions, and we were able to get me off the plane without any trouble. And I didn't have any trouble

79

with the written exam. By this time, my right hand was virtually useless for writing, but my writing with my left hand was legible enough for a test that would have required more writing than this one did. It turned out to be a multiple-choice test. No problem. I dreaded the thought of the flight back to Chicago, but the word about me must have traveled through the whole airline company. Again no problems. We were back home in Lynbrook in a few hours, I was now on my way to becoming a certified specialist in rehabilitation medicine.

At the time I had been given the fellowship to the institute, I notified the administrator of Mary Immaculate Hospital, where I had worked in anesthesia for so long, that I was taking a three-year leave of absence. I preferred this to resigning from the staff because I loved the hospital and hoped to work there again someday. Two years later, after I had been working at Beth Israel for a few months, I got a call from Mary Immaculate, asking me to stop by to discuss some plans the hospital had. The plans: Mary Immaculate had a small rehab facility which they now wanted to expand. Would I do the same job at Mary Immaculate that I had done at Beth Israel? And would I become director of the unit? By all means.

Then, as I was completing my residency, which had been shortened by six months because I was given one half year's credit for my previous experience, Dr. Bernice Clark, the director of the outpatients' services, called me into her office and said: "Joe, I've spoken to Dr. Rusk, and both he and I would like you to stay on in the Outpatient Department as an attending physician on a part-time basis. You will also be given a faculty appointment and part of your duties will be teaching residents who rotate through the outpatient service. Most of your work will be in the Specialized Services Unit with Dr. Allan Russek. What do you say?"

All of a sudden I had three jobs. The future that had looked so bleak not long ago was suddenly crammed with activity. From feeling helpless and hopeless, I suddenly felt useful and needed and of value.

And what made me feel of special value was that I was now working with patients whose conditions and problems and attitudes I could understand because I had gone through them myself. I was still going through them. So, as I worked with more and more handicapped patients, I developed a better understanding of myself as well as of them.

Rehabilitation medicine has been around ever since the beginning of medicine. The earliest medical practitioners knew there were therapeutic values in the sun and water, in heat and cold, in exercise, in prosthetic devices. The challenge was to establish what to use for the disabled, how, and when. Like all of medicine, rehabilitation medicine has progressed more in the past hundred years than in all the centuries before, and, ironically, much of the progress has been the result of the urgencies of wars. The greatest strides were the products of World War II. When I was in medical school, we had lectures on physical medicine, but they were more on the physical modalities than on the practice of the specialty medicine itself. Learning this aspect of rehabilitation medicine took up more of my time during my residency at the institute than anything else. And I also learned that there was more than the physical involved. The total-man concept philosophy of Dr. Rusk became even more important and fundamental as I became more knowledgeable in this specialty.

Whether I was working at the institute, Beth Israel, Mary Immaculate or any of the other hospitals where I subsequently worked, a day rarely passed without an experience that bothered me at first, until I got used to it. A patient would be brought to me to be evaluated, he would see me in my wheelchair, eventually unable to use my arms, and he would ask himself: "If this guy is in such bad shape himself, how come he thinks he can help me?" With the question would come a hesitancy to communicate, a resentment to the touches and feels of the assistant working with me and a generally negative attitude that could take the value out of my medical supervision.

Time and again, I had to say to such patients: "Look, your

life isn't over. Maybe you can't do some of the things you used to do, but you've still got a lot to live for. You can conquer this. I did it; and if I did it, you can do it."

The disability that is suddenly acquired, from accidents, perhaps, is without question the most difficult for people to accept, especially young people. Usually there is the question "Why me?" Sometimes there is the question "Can I get better?" And sometimes there is the question "Can you help me get better?" With physical disabilities, the patient can do more to make himself better than anybody else can, but he has got to want to. With physical disabilities, I have learned—and watched others learn—that fighters live and quitters die. With physical disabilities, the death isn't actual death, at least not right away. It is a living death of deepening bitterness, deepening hopelessness, the loss of drive and dreams. A patient in this condition can have a depressing effect on the entire staff. A fighter has the directly opposite effect.

For example, Manny, a construction worker, was twenty-seven when one day a wall caved in on him, causing multiple internal injuries and requiring the amputation of both legs above the knees. He underwent several operations to correct the multiple injuries, requiring many transfusions. He had a stormy convalescence which left him emaciated and dehabilitated. When he was brought over to our rehabilitation facility, he was still not completely recovered from his post-surgical complications. He was a Portuguese and spoke no English. We had to have his wife with us during examinations to do the translating.

During an early evaluation, Manny was told that his chances were guarded. But if he were to work hard, he would have a fair chance of walking again. He would have to undergo further surgery to prepare his stumps for prosthetic devices. We would start him out with simple devices—peg legs, actually—slowly progressing to the more sophisticated artificial limbs.

And I warned: "This is going to take a long time, it will be difficult and it can be very painful. It's up to you."

Manny's wife translated, he listened, he thought about it, then he said something, and his wife laughed.

I asked: "What did he say?"

She said: "He said he is going to walk out of this place if it is the last thing he does."

"He will," I said, "and it won't be."

The process was, indeed, slow, difficult and painful, but Manny never complained, he never wasted a minute during therapy and he was always ready for whatever he had to do next. Often what he had to do was mental as well as physical. He had to keep in mind that he was, in a sense, walking on air, that the part of him that touched the floor wasn't really him. He had to learn to walk more with his thighs than his feet. He had to develop a new sense of balance, and he had to build up his confidence in it. And throughout the process he had to work with people who could communicate with him only in sign language. But finally one day we all watched Manny walk out of the hospital, and we all cheered him. He had won his fight.

Another good fighter was Mrs. Carroll, a young wife and mother who had developed transverse myelitis, which paralyzed her from the waist down. She was in very low spirits when she first came to us. Although patients were expected to follow the routines we set for them, we knew that often patients needed a period of adjustment before they could get into the swing of things, and though we didn't leave them alone, we didn't push them. Mrs. Carroll's first signs of interest appeared during the psychological sessions, individual and group, that we had made part of our therapy. Mrs. Carroll was a well-educated woman, and she seemed to have a better grasp of psychotherapy than many people have.

During a group session one day, Mrs. Carroll said to the psychologist: "Doctor, there is a subject we seem to be avoiding. Sexual relationships. What kind of a sex life can a paralyzed person expect to have? And how do we adjust to the possibility of not having any? I think that's an important subject."

"I do, too," the psychologist said.

And that was how we started a sex education course as part of our therapy. Of course, the situation varied from patient to patient and, in each case, the physician and the psychologist worked together to prepare each patient for the future. But at last the subject was out in the open, and we soon saw that the new program was achieving a lot of good.

This seemed to be a turning point for Mrs. Carroll, and she took up the physical side of her therapy in good spirits. One day during an examination, she said to me: "Doctor, I have a wonderful husband and two fine children. I refuse to spend the rest of my life having them wait on me. You have got to teach me how to get around."

"We can teach you," I said, "but you're the one who's got to do the learning."

Mrs. Carroll was ready to go home in a few months. She was able to take care of her home herself, including the cooking and cleaning, with the help of crutches and canes, and she used her wheelchair only when traveling some distance or when she knew she would be in a crowded place. We always encouraged our patients to stay in touch with us after their release from the hospital, in case they had any problems. We never heard from Mrs. Carroll after that, so presumably she had no problems.

The effect of a disability on a marriage depends entirely on the two people involved. If it was a good marriage to begin with and, especially, if the man and woman have a solid religious foundation, there usually aren't any threatening problems. And yet I have seen a disability put an end to a marriage. I've observed that wives are more willing to stay with a disabled husband than husbands are willing to stay with disabled wives. If the wife has to go out to work to support the family, certain risks obviously arise, but what happens depends entirely on the woman. The husband would be going out to work anyway, and what happens to him depends a great deal on how willing he is to face the fact that when his day's work ends his day's work may not be over. He may have to do chores that his wife can no longer do if there is no one else to do them. He may have to look after small children. His social life may be cut down. His sex life may be cut off because he fears and is ignorant of the sexual desires of his disabled wife. Counseling can help a marriage endangered by a serious physical disability. But nothing can help better than a solid religious foundation shared by the married couple.

A close friend of the family for years has been a Franciscan teaching brother who taught at St. Francis College while I was a student there, and he came to know Jo because she was often at the college helping me run various activities. The friendship grew better as the years passed and the family was always glad when the brother could come to the house for dinner.

One evening when he was with us, he asked: "Joe, do you know the difference between heaven and hell?"

"I think so," I said. "One place is hot and the other is cool." The kids laughed at my inadvertently hip talk.

"Well, that's true," he said. "But there's something else. All the people in hell are surrounded by long tables that are loaded with wonderful food, the most delicious food in the world, but all the people in hell are miserable."

"Why?"

"Because they have permanently stiffened arms and they cannot eat."

"And what about heaven?"

"Well," he said, "all the people in heaven are also surrounded by long tables loaded with wonderful food, the most delicious food in the world. All the people in heaven also have permanently stiffened arms, but they are perfectly happy."

I asked: "How come?"

He said: "They feed each other."

That made me think of myself, of my work, of my patients, of all the handicapped people in the world, who, like me, need others to feed us in one way or another.

An attitude that often strikes recently and suddenly disabled people, especially the young, is that because they have lost certain physical abilities they have also lost a certain physical attractiveness. They begin to consider themselves unlovable, and the longer they feel this way the more likely they are to stop being self-loving. It becomes extremely difficult to treat a disabled person who doesn't see any reason for bothering. What good would he be to anybody? Who would want him?

A case in point was Jimmy, just twenty, who had been in a motorcycle accident and was left paralyzed from the waist down. By the time he came to us, he had already quit life. He went to physical therapy sessions because he knew he had to, but he participated halfheartedly. He went to group therapy because he knew that this, too, was required of him, but he didn't participate at all. He made no friends in his ward and he rebuffed the overtures of others. He told his family that he didn't want visitors.

We were discussing Jimmy one day at a staff meeting, and the psychiatrist said: "What has happened to Jimmy is totally clear. He is paralyzed, his love life is over at twenty, he is convinced that no girl would ever become interested in him again. Why should she?"

I thought about that. I turned to the head nurse and asked: "How many nurses work in Jimmy's ward during the day?"

"Four."

"Are they young and pretty?"

She looked surprised. "Yes, they're young, and I suppose a couple of them are pretty."

"Good," I said. "Please tell them what I want them to do. I want them to pay extra attention to Jimmy. Chat with him a few minutes a day. Tell him how good he looks and how well he's doing. Tell them not to go overboard—he'd see through that. Just tell them to treat him like he was a boy they'd just met and liked and wanted to know better. Get him to talk about himself. Jimmy told me that he plays the guitar. Have his parents bring it in. And tell the nurses to ask him to play for them once in a while."

In 1967 Joe was presented the Presidential Citation for Meritorious Service for Employment of the Handicapped. From left to right are J. Victor Herd, president of Continental Insurance Co.; Dr. Henry Viscardi, founder of Human Resources; Joe, Jo and Jeffrey.

Working at home with help from James, 1969. (Credit: Bob West)

Joe with Dr. Frank Field on NBC's "Project Research," November 14, 1971. (Credit: NBC-TV)

June 4, 1977, Joe was awarded an honorary degree of Doctor of Science by Brother Donald Sullivan, O.S.F., president of St. Francis College (left). They were joined by Bishop Francis J. Mugavero, D.D.

Mrs. Rosalynn Carter presents the Handicapped American of 1976 Award from the Presidential Committee on the Employment of the Handicapped to Joe and Jo, May 1977. (Credit: Official Photo, The White House)

The head nurse said: "Won't the guitar bother some of the other patients?"

"They'll probably enjoy it, too," I said. "We've got to build up the boy's ego if we hope to build up his body."

"But," she said, "suppose Jimmy becomes emotionally involved with one of the nurses? How are we going to handle that?"

"I don't think that will happen," I said. "I'm sure Jimmy had plenty of girl friends before the accident. He just has to feel that he's going to have them when he goes home."

It worked like a charm. In a week Jimmy was the first person to show up for his physical therapy sessions. During his rest periods, he'd go back to the equipment and work by himself or he'd go to the pool. I got used to hearing his guitar playing down the hall. I got used to hearing his laughter. When he left, Jimmy could maneuver very well on his crutches. He would never be able to walk on his own two feet again, but he would be able to love and accept love because he had relearned how to love himself.

If there is any miracle in rehabilitation medicine, it is love. In a sense, the handicapped person needs to be able to feed others love as much as he needs to be lovingly fed himself. I witnessed a beautiful example of this one day at Beth Israel. The patient was an elderly woman whose experiences in a Nazi prison camp had left her with a slowly but steadily advancing paralysis of the upper extremities. At this point, her arms were almost as lifeless as mine.

I was evaluating her one day when, with tears in her eyes, she said: "Dr. Yussef, you have got to save my arms. I want to be able to hug my grandchildren."

I thought to myself: "So do I."

My children were bringing home cats and dogs, but as yet they hadn't brought home any grandchildren. I wasn't expecting that—they were all still too young. Those who were old enough to be aware of me when I was able to get around on my own had only vague memories of it. None of them ever gave any sign of being uneasy or embarrassed by my condition. For all I knew, they never mentioned me to their new friends when they brought them home for the first time. I had to assume this because more than once I saw a new friend do a double take when he caught sight of me in my wheelchair.

Jo and I always hoped that none of our children would get married before finishing college. This way, we felt, in case anything happened to them, they wouldn't have to resort to menial jobs to earn a living. So far, we've been lucky.

Jeanine got a degree in nursing and worked for a year before marrying Joseph Sanfilippo, who worked for a Wall Street investment firm. Joseph got a decree in sociology, then started his own business of producing handcrafted items before marrying Jane, who was a teacher and worked with exceptional children. Jacqueline became a teacher, majoring in art, and then married her high school sweetheart, Richard Safrath, who had become a policeman. Jennifer became an elementary school teacher and then married Joseph Villacci, an prosthetist manufacturing braces and limbs. Jeff became a dental technician. Judy received a bachelor of science degree in animal science and has decided on graduate work. James, who came along eight years after Judy, at a time when Jo and I thought our child-producing era was over, is a teen-ager at this point—very active in baseball, water sports, skiing and boating—and hasn't indicated what he wants to do with his life except enjoy it.

As my family continued to grow and grow older, my career continued to grow. I was at Beth Israel Hospital, Mary Immaculate Hospital and at the institute working in the Outpatient Department and sharing an office with Dr. Russek, from whom I acquired a thorough basic knowledge of artificial limbs and back problems. In 1960, I received a call from the superintendent of St. Mary's Hospital, where I had interned, asking me if I would be interested in setting up a Department of Physical Rehabilitation Medicine. Having had such strong ties to the hospital, I could not say no. This caused me to put in longer and longer hours of work, going from hospital to hospital, but I was doing what I loved best—building and developing facilities for the disabled.

At the same time, an orthopedic surgeon, for whom I had given countless anesthesias at Mary Immaculate, called me and asked if I would set up a department at Jamaica Hospital. Although I was very busy, I said yes, having the utmost respect and admiration for Dr. Fred Courten, who had always been good to me in the operating room. Jamaica Hospital presented quite a challenge at that time because of the lack of space. However, with hard work we were able to overcome many obstacles and soon the department became a very busy facility.

In the meantime, I was busy giving lectures and speeches to various groups. The more I learned and understood about the handicapped, the more I wanted to do whatever I could to help them—help us, I suppose—so I never missed an opportunity to spread the word on behalf of the handicapped.

I also felt that the more visible a handicapped person was, the easier it would be for society to be comfortable with the disabled. I made it a practice to attend meetings and conventions where there would be other doctors who were not aware of the disabled. I attended A.M.A. conventions where I was the only disabled doctor present. I could see the startled look of other physicians who wondered how a disabled person could perform in medicine. I think one of the most surprising incidents occurred when the A.M.A. had its meeting in Miami and I attended in force—not only with my wife and all seven children but also my mother and father. Within a day or two of the convention, we could sense that there had been considerable talk about the disabled doctor who had brought his whole family with him, so much so that a photographer called from the *Medical Tribune* asking for an interview and pictures of the entire family. The story even made the local papers. Good-naturedly, many people stopped to ask if we had chartered a plane, and surprisingly many doctors asked questions about the disabled and modes of travel. It made me feel good that the disabled were getting some favorable exposure. Besides, my family was having a wonderful time.

In 1962, Dr. Rusk asked me to see him. At the time, the Continental Insurance Company was a leading insurer in the compensation and liability area, insuring many industries where there was a risk of on-the-job injuries to employees who would then become in need of rehabilitation therapy. Dr. Fred Schilling, Medical Director and Vice-President at Continental, wanted to set up a rehabilitation department where the compensation claims could be evaluated for possible need of early rehabilitation treatment and, if the patient was receiving treatment, evaluating whether or not it was the proper treatment and whether more effective procedures should be recommended. Dr. Schilling had asked Dr. Rusk to recommend someone for the job.

Dr. Rusk said to me: "Joe, I know you can do this job. It's going to take up a lot of your time, and you may have to give up some of the other things you are doing."

"I wouldn't know what to give up," I admitted. "I like everything I'm doing."

"Well, Joe," he said, "I hope you won't give up the institute. We need you around here. But this job at Continental is important. It's a developing idea. The insurance industry is becoming aware of its community responsibility. And it can mean as much to the patient as it can to the insurance business. As far as I'm concerned, you're the best man for the job."

Being told that by the man who had become my hero in medicine settled the matter for me. I had an interview with Dr. Schilling and I took the job. It was, as Dr. Rusk had warned, a very demanding job that took up a lot of my time.

For several months, I had frequent meetings with Dr. Schilling and top executives of the company as we discussed pros and cons of the program and worked out guidelines. Finally we were ready to launch the program. A notice went out to all claims supervisors that the company had gone into this field, and the supervisors were requested to attend a seminar at the home office. Dr. Schilling and I and other members of the medical department worked out a two-day study program, and then we were on the way.

Something I had not foreseen was the amount of traveling I would have to do for the company. This became both a wonderful and tiring task. At about this time, various other companies were also becoming interested in rehabilitation, and one day I was invited to meet with the executives of several large insurance companies. Out of the meeting came a group known as the Insurance Rehabilitation Study Committee. At first, there were twelve companies involved; today there are around thirty. In 1966, I was honored by being elected chairman of the committee for that year. The goal of the group was to develop ways to provide early rehabilitation which could decrease a disability and, hopefully, return the patient to gainful employment. The committee met two or three times a year in various parts of the country I otherwise would probably never have seen.

This traveling provided a real bonus for our children. Jo and I made it a practice to take one or two of the children with us on all our trips. To this day, at family meetings, which occur practically every day, the kids, most of them now parents, love to talk about the fun they had on those trips.

But there was something else to consider. As Dr. Rusk had forewarned, I simply did not have the time to remain with the hospitals where I was working. Deciding which positions to give up was extremely difficult. Working with me was Dr. Marie Sortino, who had been trained at NYU, and I asked her if she would be interested in the position at St. Mary's. She said yes. So I was able to withdraw from St. Mary's. Withdrawing from Beth Israel was painful. It had been my first job. But I had to. There just wasn't time.

But more than time was involved. My multiple sclerosis was advancing and I was having more and more trouble taking care of myself. My right arm was almost completely gone and my left arm deteriorating slowly. I had increasing difficulty eating. I had to bend low to bring the food to my mouth. Even so, food fell off the fork. A spoon of soup landed on the tablecloth. I couldn't cut the meat. One morning, I was unable to shave myself. As each faculty left me, Jo took over, feeding me. The first time she shaved me, she said: "If I turn out to be any good at this, I'm going to get myself a job in your father's barbershop."

I couldn't drive anymore. I knew I couldn't rely on Jo to drive me everywhere I had to go. She had a home to run, kids to raise, so I had to find somebody else. Working at Mary Immaculate was a young man who was always very helpful to me. I offered him the job as my personal attendant and driver, and he accepted.

In a way, it was an easy job, and yet it had several drawbacks. The attendant had to be at my house by seven in the morning in order to get me to my first appointment, usually around eight. By the time he arrived, Jo had me up, shaved, dressed and fed. Then he had to get me from my wheelchair into the car. At first, he had to lift me, so he had to be strong. Later on I had a hoisting device installed in the car. This was a hydraulic lift known as the Hoyer Car Lift. At the car, the attendant had to attach chains of the lift to a canvas on which I was sitting in the wheelchair. Then he had to work the controls to hoist me up and swing me to the car. Then he had to align my body so that when he lowered me I would be comfortable in the seat. Then he would adjust the seat belt. At our destination, we went through the reverse. Sometimes I had two or three stops to make in a day, each time going through the same process. Often we drew crowds.

While I'd be working at the insurance company or a hospital, there would be nothing for the attendant to do. If he was a reader, he had plenty of time for it. Otherwise, the job could become very boring.

Usually I had lunch brought in and my attendant would feed me. This gets some people a little nervous, and often I had a Coke spilled on me or I nipped the attendant's fingers as I tried to bite into a sandwich.

Toileting was really not a problem. My wife and I would take care of my bowel movements on a regular routine at home. I always made arrangements for my attendant to be nearby so I could use a urinal while at work. When I was traveling on a long trip, I resorted to receptacles I wore for these functions.

Not surprisingly, I had trouble keeping attendants. Often we didn't get back to my house until seven or eight at night, late enough to deprive the attendant of his own evening. They kept quitting on me. Late in 1968, when my son Jeff finished his training as a dental technician, he offered to work as my attendant and driver for a while until I could find a man who gave a bit more evidence of permanency. It worked out very well. First, Jeff and I lived in the same house and he could help Jo get me ready for the day every morning. Sometimes when an attendant would be late arriving to pick me up, I'd fret because I knew I'd be running late all day. With Jeff, this was no problem. The only problem was getting him out of bed in the morning. Jeff also had no problem about what to do with himself while I was working. He loved to socialize with the patients and many times he would act as a go-between for the patients, with me or with the staff. Jeff also loved to eat. He had me spending more money on his lunch than most people spend on a complete dinner. From time to time, as he concentrated on his own lunch, I had to say: "Jeff, how about feeding me something?" Jeff grew into a tall, heavy-set young man—close to fat—but he had the strength so that my own weight was no problem for him whenever he had to lift me. He was also very affable, with a wonderful sense of humor. He liked people. He would wander around the insurance office or the hospital and visit with people. He had a lot of friends. Around the hospital, Jeff was helpful to me in an unusual way. With his outgoing personality, he easily won the confidence of young people who had become disabled. If there was something troubling a patient that he couldn't bring himself to talk to me about, he would tell Jeff, knowing Jeff would tell me. Next time I saw the patient, I was able to be more specifically effective in the treatment than I might otherwise have been. My only complaint with Jeff was that, although he was a good driver, he was a fast driver. When you are sitting there helpless next to a speed king, you don't feel very safe. I often had to tell him to slow down. Evenings after dinner, he'd go out with his friends and usually I didn't see him again until morning.

Because we spent so much time together, I probably grew closer to Jeff than I was to the other children. I was so dependent upon him. He seemed to enjoy the job. Months passed, years passed, and Jeff gave no indication of wanting to start off on his own career. He always referred to me as "my Daddy." I always had to laugh when I would hear him step out into a corridor and tell an insurance executive or a hospital administrator: "My Daddy would like to see you."

My own father died in 1971 at the age of eighty-one, from renal complications. He died rather suddenly. He had been active up until the day before he was admitted to the hospital. His death was so sudden and so unexpected that we were all still in a state of shock when, three weeks later, my mother, who was staying with us, suffered a massive cerebral vascular accident. One night my daughter Judy, who had been setting her hair, heard a strange noise coming from the bathroom. She looked in and saw my mother slumped over and unconscious. Judy immediately called us, and two weeks later, after having all kinds of medical emergency treatment, my mother passed away without regaining consciousness. The double shock of losing both parents in such a short time was a severe blow to the family. If it hadn't been for the demands of my work, I'm not sure yet how I would have survived the experience. Time passed, helpfully.

On Thursday, November 9, 1972, Jeff and I got home around seven. We had dinner with the family and then Jeff went out. Jo and I had some husband and wife talk for a while and then we watched some television, and around eleven Jo helped me get into bed. As she was preparing herself for bed, I became aware of a pain in my chest. I decided not to mention it. A few years previous, I'd had a heart attack, not severe but bad enough to put me out of action for a month. Now my pain grew worse.

I had to say: "Babe, I've got the darnedest pain in my chest."

She looked at me anxiously. "Where in your chest?"

"All over."

"What about your arms?"

"No."

"I'm going to call the doctor."

She called a friend who usually took care of the family's ills, and he said: "Sounds like a heart attack, Jo. Get him over to Franklin General. I'll meet you there."

It was November and the nights were chilly. Jo was putting some clothes on me when Jeff came home.

"What's the matter?" he asked.

Jo said: "The doctor thinks Dad is having a heart attack. We've got to get him to the hospital."

Jeff helped Jo dress me, then he said: "I'll get the car."

Jo said: "I don't think we should use the car. I'll call the police department and get an ambulance."

The ambulance arrived in a few minutes. When Jeff saw that the two attendants were having difficulty lifting me from the bed to the stretcher, he said: "I'll help my Daddy." And he got me onto the stretcher. Then he helped the attendants carry me to the ambulance.

I was put into the ambulance. Jo got in; so did an attendant. Jeff tried to get in, but the attendant said: "Sorry. Only one person can get in."

Jeff said: "I'll take the car."

Judy came to the door and said: "Jeff, wait for me. I'll get a coat. I want to go with you."

"No," Jeff said. "You stay here with Jennifer. And call Jeanine and Jackie and Joseph and tell them Daddy has had a heart attack."

The ambulance was at the hospital in a few minutes. The doctor was waiting for me. After examining me, he instructed the nurse to transfer me to the Cardiac Care Unit. The sedative I had received was beginning to take effect and I began to drift off to sleep. As I was being wheeled through the emergency room, I heard a young man talking in a loud, excited voice to the ambulance attendants about a terrible car accident which had just happened about a block away from the hospital.

As Jo filled out the admittance forms, she kept wondering where Jeff was. From time to time, she went to a window and looked out at the parking lot. She called the house.

Judy said: "Jeff left right after you did. He should be there by now."

"He isn't," Jo said, starting to worry.

When Jo was allowed to see me, I asked: "Where's Jeff?"

"He'll be here any minute," she said. But he wasn't.

As soon as she had to leave my room, Jo called the house again. Nobody knew where Jeff was.

Jo had been at the hospital about an hour when she was asked to go downstairs to a waiting room near the emergency room. There she saw my doctor, who told her that the two men with him were plainclothes detectives and they had something to tell her.

One of the detectives asked: "Are you Mrs. Panzarella?"

"Yes, I am," she said.

Before the detective could say anything, Jo intuitively knew that something had happened to Jeff. She heard the detective say: "We have some very bad news for you."

Jo said: "It's Jeff, isn't it?"

"Yes, ma'am."

Jo broke down momentarily and the detective held her. Then he told her that, in his rush to get to the hospital, Jeff either lost control of the car or the car went out of control—we will never know—and crashed into a telephone pole about a block from the hospital. The car was demolished and Jeffrey was killed instantly.

The second detective said: "It will be necessary for somebody to identify the body."

Jo nodded. "All right. I will."

The man said: "Mrs. Panzarella, I don't think you should be the one to do this. Your son was very badly injured."

Jo said: "Then I'll call my brother-in-law. I'm sure he will be here in a few minutes."

By the time he arrived, a Malverne policeman, who was a good friend of my son's, had already identified Jeff, and he was taken to the Nassau County Medical Center morgue.

Jo called home again and told Judy and Jennifer what had happened.

The girls had called Jeanine, then living in New Jersey, and she and her husband Joe headed to Lynbrook right away. Jackie and Richie came in from Babylon. Joseph and his wife were living in our summer home on Long Island at Setauket while Jane was taking graduate courses at the nearby State University at Stony Brook. Earlier that evening, a storm had knocked out the telephone service in the Setauket neighborhood, and the girls could not reach Joseph. Jo mentioned this to the detectives at the hospital, and they called the Suffolk County Police and had someone go to the house and tell Joseph to call his parents. Joseph and Jane had to go into town to find a pay phone. Joseph was so overwrought by the news that Jane drove him into Lynbrook, both of them still in their nightclothes.

After a while, Jo was allowed to see me again, but I was under such strong sedation that I was only vaguely aware of her. The doctor advised Jo to go home and get some rest. Ed drove her home, wisely avoiding the wrecked car, splintered around a telephone pole a few hundred feet from the hospital.

When they were all together, Jo and the children held a family conference. Jo said: "Your father cannot be told about Jeff, not yet. The doctor said we shouldn't tell him, and I agree. We probably can start visiting Dad sometime tomorrow, and he will ask about Jeff, so we will all have to agree each day on the reason Jeff isn't there."

The visits began the next afternoon. First Jo came in for five minutes, then Jeanine and Jacqueline for five minutes, the time being limited because I was still in the Coronary Care Unit. Then Jo again.

I asked: "Where's Jeff?"

She said: "Well, Jeff felt that the other children should see you first."

I said: "That sounds like Jeff."

That night was the first evening of the wake. Because Jeff had been so disfigured, the coffin was kept closed. The funeral parlor was jammed, and a long line made its way outside and down the block. Jo had no idea that Jeff had so many friends. Many of the visitors were former patients of mine, some in wheelchairs or on crutches, and they told Jo how much they had loved Jeffrey, how he had encouraged them and inspired them during the bleak periods early in their disabilities. None of us in the family had known anything about that.

The next afternoon, when the visiting resumed, Jo came in first. Then Joseph. Then Jennifer and Judy. Then Jo again.

I asked: "Where's Jeff?"

She said: "Something came up. He had to go somewhere. He'll try to get here later."

That didn't sound like Jeff. I was sure nothing would keep him from his Daddy in these circumstances.

That night the funeral parlor was again packed, and again there was the long line outside.

The next afternoon, again there was no Jeffrey. I asked Jo: "Where's Jeff? Why doesn't Jeff come to see me?"

She said: "Honey, Jeff has caught a cold and he doesn't want to come and see you because he doesn't want you to catch it."

"All right."

That evening, a young priest came up to Jo and said: "Mrs. Panzarella, Jeff and I and a few other fellows have been working with a youth group. Some of the boys and girls are here tonight, and they would like to make a statement about the things Jeff did for them. Would that be all right?"

"Yes, of course."

So the parade of love began. The boys and girls, ranging from twelve to sixteen, all came forward in a group in front of the coffin and faced the mourners and told what Jeff had done for them. They told how Jeff had planned—and was in the process of setting up—a youth club where they could engage in sports and other activities that would give them something to do and keep them off the streets. They affectionately referred to him as "Big Daddy." They told how generous he was and how many times he gave them money for things they themselves could not afford, and that he was always available to help when help was needed. Jo could not believe her ears.

Arrangements had been made to bury Jeff in the same plot with my parents, but that night at home Jo told the family: "I'm sure that by tomorrow your father will realize that something has happened to Jeff. He keeps asking about Jeff, and we can't put this off any longer. Besides, I am not going to let Jeff be buried until your father knows that Jeff is dead."

With that, Jo called my doctor and told him that the time had come for me to be told. She also called an old friend of ours, Father Harth, and he said he would be present when I was told. Two close medical friends offered to be nearby in case they were needed.

When the question arose about who should tell me, Joseph said: "I'll tell Daddy, Mom."

The next afternoon, just before visiting hours, a nurse gave me an injection. I wondered why she should do that just before I was expecting my family. Then Jo, Joseph and Jane, and Father Harth came into the room. I sensed something was wrong.

When I didn't see Jeff, I said: "What's the matter? What's happened to Jeff?"

Joseph said: "Dad, the night you had the heart attack, Jeff followed the ambulance to the hospital in the car. There was an accident. Jeff was killed, Dad."

"Oh, God," was all I could say. I cried. I would never see my son again. I couldn't speak for a long time. We were all in tears, and Father Harth tried to comfort us. Finally I asked what arrangements had been made for Jeff.

Jo said: "We're planning on burying Jeff in the same plot with your parents."

"No," I said. "I want Jeff to have his own plot. I want Jeff to be with us."

After the funeral, the family told me everything. The accident. How Jo dressed in bright and gay clothes to visit me in the hospital, then rushed home to change into clothes for the wake. The crowds at the funeral parlor. The former patients. The youngsters giving their testimonies about how Jeff had helped them, one after another.

So I did not really get to know my son until after he had died. After he was dead, I discovered that he had spent his life helping others, feeding others, in one way or another.

I knew now that I had to get well. I knew that I had to get back to work. I knew that I had to go on helping the handicapped, helping them in one way or another.

Jeff would have wanted that.

My daughter Jeanine was working in Englewood, New Jersey, as a staff nurse. When I was transferred from the Coronary Care Unit to a private room, she insisted that she become my day special while I recuperated from the heart attack in the hospital. She put in a long day, and she took complete care of me. After a few days, I noticed that Jeanine looked tired. I asked her about her health, and she said she was all right. But each day her weariness became more evident in her face and in her movements. At times I thought I saw her try to suppress pain. I mentioned this to my wife.

One day when Jo got home from the hospital, she found Jeanine in bed. Her husband Joe was nearby, and very concerned. Joe told my wife that Jeanine was most likely pregnant. He had called her physician in Englewood. Because of the distance, the doctor suggested that Jeanine be seen immediately by a doctor in our area.

Jo called a colleague of mine who interrupted his Thanksgiving dinner and came immediately. After examining Jeanine, he suggested that she be taken to an obstetrician as soon as possible. Jo called my cousin, Dr. Joseph A. Panzarella, and he wanted Jeanine brought to the hospital right away. It was difficult to get an ambulance on a holiday, but finally Jeanine got there. My cousin was waiting. After checking Jeanine's vital signs, he immediately called the operating room for emergency surgery.

After the operation, he told my wife: "That was close. Jeanine had an ectopic pregnancy and had already ruptured. Another few minutes, and we could have lost her."

That gave me a lot to think about. My son Jeffrey had given his life in his rush to help me in a critical moment in my life. My daughter Jeanine had almost given her life in her determination to help me regain my life.

Most fathers never find out how much their children love them. I have, again and again. I've got good kids, thank God.

And thank Jo.

X

Nothing like it had ever happened to me before.

As I had become more and more active in work with the handicapped and for the handicapped, I was called on more and more to give speeches, sometimes to professional groups, sometimes to lay groups, and usually some personal publicity came out of it. Personally, I was not interested in publicity for myself; but I felt that every time a reference to the handicapped appeared in the newspapers, the handicapped could benefit in one way or another. After years of being handicapped myself and working with hundreds of other people who were handicapped, I thought it was time for the handicapped to be brought out of their hiding place in a back room.

In any event, over the years certain honors were given me. In 1966, I was chosen the Outstanding Disabled Veteran in New York State. In 1967, I received a Presidential Citation for Meritorious Service for Employment of the Handicapped. In 1968, the Board of Directors of the Catholic Medical Center, Mary Immaculate Hospital, gave me a citation for outstanding service in the field of physical medicine and rehabilitation. In 1973, I received another presidential citation. Each time, there was publicity. Out of the publicity came more opportunities to give a talk or write a paper. Each time, a little of the stigma of being handicapped faded away.

Over the years I had observed that most handicapped people don't ask the world for any favors. Once a disabled person adjusts psychologically to his disability, accepts it and, when necessary, finishes his training for a different way to earn a living, all he asks is a fair chance to compete in the job market. He doesn't always get it.

For example, one of my patients incurred an on-the-job injury in the factory where he worked that left his legs paralyzed. The company was insured, so there were no problems about the costly medical bills. The man let the company know when he was ready to go back to work—in a wheelchair. He was given a desk job. The company's headquarters was eight stories high, but the elevator went up only seven floors. The man was given a desk on the eighth floor. This meant that every morning he had to be carried up the steps. When no one was available to help him, he had to exert terrific effort to maneuver himself onto the stairs and then hoist himself up, step by step. Many times, he had to go through the reverse procedure at the end of the day.

Naturally, he could not tolerate this for long and had to give up the job. Now, had somebody in the company just been thoughtless? Or had there been a conscious effort to keep the man out of sight? Or had he been presented with an obstacle course in the hope that he would quit? I know of many similar situations.

For many people, having a handicapped person around can be a source of discomfort and displeasure. Some disabled people are not pleasant to look at or their disability forces them to do certain things in a way that might be unattractive to others. I remember reading about a famous jazz musician, blind, who was refused entry in a famous Chicago restaurant because he had his Seeing Eye dog with him. Dogs weren't allowed in the place. The dog wouldn't have been any problem. Seeing Eye dogs are trained to cope with such situations. I've known blind people whose dogs would sit next to them for hours on end without moving a muscle. But the musician might have been a problem. He was alone, so the waiter would have had to tell him what was on the menu. Maybe the waiter would have to cut the meat and tell the musician at what "o'clock" the various foods were on the plate. The same with the coffee, and maybe the waiter would have to put in the cream and sugar. And maybe the man would have been a little bit sloppy. Evidently, the management felt that the customers who would have been willing to pay a lot of money to hear the musician play didn't want to have to look at him while they were eating. Variations on this theme happen a lot.

After I became a quadriplegic, I needed a little time to adjust to eating in public. First, I had to adjust to other people's eating habits. Say that personally I'd prefer to try the meat, then a bit of the salad, then some of the potato, then a bite of bread or a sip of wine, but the person feeding me preferred a different order. I just had to accept it. Usually my wife feeds me, in public and at home, and I know her well enough to be able to tell her what I want in case she neglects something. The next thing I had to adjust to was being stared at in restaurants. Time and again the low buzz of conversation would be pierced by a child's voice asking: "Mommy, why does that man have to be fed?" But we all got used to it after a while and stopped paying attention to it. That is one of the things handicapped people have to learn: If you can cope, you can conquer.

And you have to cope with some unusual things. In my case, I gradually reached the point where I had no privacy except in my thoughts. For everything else, I needed to have somebody around. I grew to dislike being alone. What if there was a fire? What if somebody called with an important message and I couldn't answer the phone? What if somebody walked in with a gun and started helping himself to the family treasures? Out of this can develop a sense of obligation that can turn a disabled person into a mental—if not actual—hermit unless he learns to accept that this is the way his life is going to be and to live with it. I've noticed that disabled people feel that they are always holding up everybody else, and perhaps we do. It takes us longer to do things, usually because we have to have so many things done for us. This is something else we have to learn to cope with.

Probably the most difficult thing for a disabled person to cope with is the attitude some people have toward the disabled. Several years ago, for example, Jo and I were invited to take a cruise with some friends. As she was arranging our reservations, Jo, as she always did on travel plans, told the ticket agent that I was in a wheelchair. This shook him up a bit and he said he would call back. When he called back, he said he couldn't accept the reservations because the doors on the elevators on the ship were too narrow for a wheelchair. I asked how wide the doors were. I would have had inches to spare. Then he said he wasn't sure whether the door to the cabin and to the bathroom would be wide enough. I suggested that he check this out. The doors were wide enough.

Then he said: "I can accept this reservation only if you will sign a release."

"A release for what?"

"A release that would relieve the company from responsibility for you in case you are hurt."

I asked: "Am I likely to get hurt?"

"Well, no," he said, "but you never know."

I was losing my patience. I said: "Let's talk about this a little. Let's say I sign the release and I go on the trip and one evening I am having dinner at a table with fifteen other people and a chandelier falls from the ceiling and injures everybody at the table. You would be willing to accept the responsibility for the other fifteen people but not for me. Is that what you're saying?"

"Yes, sir. I suppose it is."

"Why?"

"Because you are immobile."

"Thank you." I backed away from the phone. I said to my wife: "Let's forget it for now."

But the idea had been sparked, and I often thought how

nice it would be if I could take the whole family on a cruise. About a year later, a patient of mine told me that she could get group-rate tickets for the *Queen Elizabeth* on a cruise to Bermuda. Jo called the Cunard Line and told them about the wheelchair. She was assured there would be no problems whatsoever. The sailing date was during Easter vacation, and Jo had about a week to pack for seven children and ourselves, but we made it. On the trip, everybody in the crew was wonderful to us. There were, in fact, a few other passengers in wheelchairs, so evidently the ship had been designed with the disabled in mind. And there was only one uneasy moment.

At Bermuda, the *QE II* was too big to dock, so she dropped anchor out in the harbor and a tender came out for the passengers who wanted to go ashore. We all wanted to go ashore, of course. To do so, however, we had to cross from the *QE II* to the tender over a gangplank that was made of rope and wooden slats. It swung slightly horizontally and bobbed slightly vertically. I didn't like this at all. But the sea was calm and there was no wind and we had no problem except the wisp of apprehension inside me. Returning later in the day was something else. The wind had come up and the sea was choppy. The tender was like a cork in a whirlpool. Even people who could walk had trouble crossing the gangplank. I knew there was no other way for me to get back onto the *Queen* so, with my sons Joseph and Jeff and the crew close in front and in back of me—all of us praying all the way—we inched across, I knowing that if the gangplank tilted enough to send me over the side I would sink into the sea like a rock. When I was finally back aboard the *Queen*, I decided that the next time we made this trip we would drive.

Travel for the disabled is easier when you are with people who understand you and, from experience, can empathize. In 1957, for example, a Pan-American conference on rehabilitation was held in Guatemala. Dr. Rusk was able to get a grant to cover the travel expenses of the people he wanted to attend with him. I was invited to give a paper on "Spasticity and Its Management." The trip was very enjoyable, the conference was very rewarding and Jo and I had a great time. One evening Dr. Rusk called our suite and asked if we would like to go sight-seeing. We quickly said yes. That evening the person who provided me with mobility by pushing my wheelchair around downtown Guatemala City was the same person who had already provided me with mobility professionally, intellectually, emotionally and personally—Dr. Rusk.

In 1968, I was offered a wonderful opportunity in my work with the disabled. Dr. Benjamin Stein, president of the Brunswick Hospital Center, Amityville, New York, called me and asked if I would meet with him and his administrator. At the meeting, Dr. Stein told me that he was opening a rehabilitation center hospital at the center. The building had already been constructed, but it needed equipment, staff and programs for both inpatients and outpatients. In other words, the rehabilitation hospital was ready to be brought to life. Would I be interested in setting up the facility? My first impulse was to say yes, but then I felt that the challenge would be so demanding that I would have to give up my other commitments—the institute, the insurance company, the colleges where I taught, the hospitals where I was a consultant—and I was reluctant to do that. I therefore told the Steins that I would be happy to help them get their facility into operation but that I would need an assistant who could be at Brunswick when my other commitments required me to be elsewhere. They agreed. I offered the position to my associate with whom I had worked at the institute of Rehabilitation Medicine and who was already assisting me at Jamaica Hospital. He accepted.

As the Brunswick Rehabilitation Hospital took on form and life I could see that whoever would eventually supervise it would have the finest rehabilitation facility on Long Island, probably the considerable environs as well. As it turned out, the final decision was not up to me. First, Mary Immaculate Hospital became incorporated into the Catholic Medical Center, with a policy that department heads must work at the center full time. It had always been a principle with me not to put all my eggs in one basket, so I withdrew from the hospital. Just about the same time, Jamaica Hospital decided to enlarge its facility and was looking for a full-time director, and I faced the same decision. But then Dr. Brown felt that Jamaica offered him a personal challenge and opportunity, so he resigned from Brunswick to go to Jamaica. As this was happening, the pressures at the insurance company began to ease greatly as we solved the problems of the program and I had to go to the office just one day every other week. I had been teaching at three colleges; but as Brunswick became increasingly functional, we found that the students could benefit more by studying at the hospital instead of their classrooms, and this cut down on a lot of the traveling I had to do. Gradually, then, I settled down more and more at Brunswick until it became my major job and my major love.

With time, I discovered that I had a much more personal reason for being dedicated to my work, a reason much closer to home. One day in 1974, while attending the Rhinebeck Arts and Crafts show, where my son Joseph was exhibiting his handicrafts, my wife and I noticed that our daughter Jackie was walking with an unsteady gait. Jo said: "I think something is wrong with Jackie. She's obviously having trouble walking. And the other day, while we were driving to Jeanine's house, her speech was garbled and indistinct."

When we returned home, I asked Jackie how she was feeling, and she said: "Daddy, I don't know. I have queer feelings. Sometimes I can't walk straight and occasionally my vision gets blurry. It's only momentary, but it's been happening a lot lately."

I shuddered inwardly. These were the very same symptoms I had first noticed when my multiple sclerosis began. I said: "All right, honey. We'll have you examined."

I called a neurologist, who then examined Jackie, but there were no findings of multiple sclerosis that could be observed clinically. I thought back to my own experience, when for a long time my diagnosis could not be confirmed. I was worried. However, Jackie did well for several months, until

April 1975, when she started to have symptoms again. This time she was admitted to New York University Hospital, where extensive testing was done. The diagnosis eliminated the possibility of a brain tumor, but there was nothing conclusive about multiple sclerosis. But Jackie started to do very well again—so well, in fact, that we forgot about her illness.

It struck again that November. We were going to Guatemala again. Dr. Julio Castillo, the Guatemalan Minister of Health, whom I had met there in 1957 and with whom I developed a lasting friendship, had invited me to read a paper on "The Modern Trends in the Treatment of Spinal Cord Injuries" at the annual meeting of the Guatemalan Medical Association, and Jo and I were taking our son James and Jackie and her husband along. I was sitting in the car, waiting for the others, the men packing our luggage in the car for the trip to the airport, when Jo came from the house. She had tears in her eyes and she was trembling. She held up a piece of paper to me. It looked like chicken scratches.

She said: "Joe, look. Jackie was trying to write a note, but she can't write."

I said: "The trip is off. We've got to get Jackie to a hospital."

But Jackie wouldn't hear of it. She insisted that she was all right and that she wanted us to go on the trip, pointing out that if she needed any medical attention there would be plenty available at a convention of doctors and that, if she needed any personal help, Richie and James would be there. Against my better judgment, I changed my mind and we went on the trip.

The trip had its mixed blessings. The medical conference was interesting and important, and there was also time to do a lot of sightseeing. At times Jackie had great difficulty eating or walking, but she was determined that she would not miss out on any of the events arranged for us. One evening we were to attend a banquet in the hotel. Jackie wasn't feeling well, so we said we would have some food sent up to her room. Ten minutes later, when the rest of us were settling at our places in the dining room, Jackie walked in, radiant, beautiful, in complete control of herself. I was so proud of her.

One day early in 1976, I decided that I would have to have a serious talk with Jackie. I was her father, but I was also a doctor, a doctor who had multiple sclerosis. I had studied the results of all the tests Jackie had undergone and I was convinced she had multiple sclerosis. I felt she should know this so that she could prepare herself. I told her.

"I know, Daddy," she said. "I accept it."

I said: "One of the problems with this disease is that you never know how long it may lie dormant, when it will flare up or how far it will go."

"I know that, too," she said. "I am your daughter, you know."

Now came the rough part. "There's something else," I said. "The general feeling in medicine is that women who have multiple sclerosis shouldn't become pregnant. There are so many risks involved. It's better not to take the chance."

Jackie's eyes filled with tears. She said: "You didn't let this beat you, and I'm not going to let it beat me. I had to wait five years to marry the man I love because you and Mom wanted me to finish college first. Well, we're married now and we're very much in love and we want a family of our own. So we're going to keep trying. If I become pregnant, I'm going to turn the baby's life over to God, just as I'm turning my life over to Him now, and just as you did twenty-five years ago."

I didn't know what to say.

Jackie went on: "You've lived with this, Dad. I can live with it. The only regret I'll have is if my hands go and I can't paint anymore. You know how I love my artwork. But I'll live with it, just as you and Mom have lived without being able to dance together."

The morning in May 1977 when we drove down to Washington, D.C., for me to receive the Presidential Award as the Handicapped American of the Year, Jackie's husband, Richie, was doing the driving. In the back seat were Jo and our son James and Jackie. Jackie was holding in her arms her beautiful new daughter, Farrah.

I thought about these things as I sat on the platform at the Washington Hilton Hotel and listened to the wife of the President of the United States talking about me. She mentioned my jobs—Brunswick, Franklin General, Continental Insurance, the three colleges—and then she looked up from her script and asked: "How does he do it?"

I knew how I did it—the only way it could have been done.

Her speech finished, Mrs. Carter presented the award. Jo accepted it. A lot of pictures were taken. Then it was my turn to speak. I had memorized my speech, but suddenly I wasn't so sure of myself. I whispered to Jo: "Babe, hold the script up for me, just in case my mind goes blank."

I began, my voice a bit unsteady. First I thanked everybody for making the award possible. Then:

"It is difficult for me to describe my emotions at this time. I am filled with happiness, and yet my happiness is tinged with sadness. I am sad because my parents, who came to this country as poor immigrants but with determination and desire to see their children achieve goals which they themselves could not attain because of circumstances, are not here today. They lived to see my sister and me achieve their goals, but today would have been the ultimate justification for all their sacrifices.

"I am also sad because my son Jeffrey, who literally gave his life for me when he was killed in an auto accident following the ambulance that was taking me to a hospital, is not here with me today. I am sure, however, that somewhere up above he is looking down with his big infectious grin, as proud as punch, and saying: 'That's my Daddy!'"

Suddenly, there was a tremendous wave of applause. When I could, I went on.

"On the other hand, I am very happy—happy because my friends, my colleagues, my relatives, my children with their respective spouses, and my grandchildren are here to share in this momentous occasion in my life."

On this, my son and three of my sons-in-law lifted their new babies high into the air. There was a cheer from the audience. Mrs. Carter laughed and waved at the babies. Then I went on to something that was very important to me.

"I also feel it is very appropriate that my wife is sitting beside me as I receive this award. It is because of her faithful and loving devotion and her determination that I am here today. Throughout the years, since my disability, she has never allowed me to lose my dignity as an individual and my role as the head of the family. She has always made sure that there would be the necessary support to allow me to overcome the obstacles imposed by my disability. She never allowed me to accept defeat despite almost insurmountable odds. With her at my side, I am happy to share this great tribute. It really belongs to her as well as to me."

This time, the ovation was for Jo. There was one more thing I wanted to say.

"I have often made the statement that the handicapped are the most discriminated against group among the minorities. Although there is no question that we have made great gains in eliminating physical barriers, we still, as disabled people, have many invisible barriers to overcome. We must break down the barriers of ignorance and fear, intolerance and indifference that have blocked the disabled from assuming their rightful place in society. All we disabled want is the chance to compete without further handicaps. We should not expect favors, just the opportunity to prove our capability. We cannot expect others to fight for our cause. We ourselves must be the leaders in eliminating these barriers to prove, by both concept and principle, that we belong in the mainstream of life.

"Let me again express my thanks and appreciation to you all for making this day the fulfillment of my most impossible dream. I am amongst all men most truly blest."

This time, it was a standing ovation. The first row of the

audience was reserved for deaf people so that they could be close enough to read the sign language that was being used as a translation by a young woman standing at my side. Suddenly all the deaf people began making the same sign with their hands. I asked the translator: "What are they saying?"

She said: "They are giving you the 'love' sign."

I was overwhelmed.

Later, off stage, Mrs. Carter stayed for a few minutes and talked with Jo about grandchildren. Congressman Otis Pike, who represented our district, came in. So did Mary Ann Krupsak, the lieutenant governor of New York State, who had come down from Albany for the presentation.

I was overwhelmed.

Then we all went to the luncheon banquet that was given by the National Multiple Sclerosis Society. People kept coming up to me, congratulating me. The experience was dazzling. The rest of my day went to interviews with the media from all over the country. All I hoped was that somewhere some disabled person would hear about all this and acquire the courage and determination to do the same for himself.

Early the next morning, I had to be at a radio station for another interview. During it, Jo waited out in the corridor. A man approached her and identified himself as being on the station's staff and also on the committee of the Washington chapter of the Multiple Sclerosis Society. He told her that a Sports Celebrity Banquet was being held that evening at our hotel, and he invited the whole family to attend.

Jo said: "I'm sorry, but we have a dinner engagement for this evening. Besides, I'm sure my husband is exhausted at this point."

"May I ask him anyway?" the man said.

"By all means."

When I came out of the studio, the man said to me: "Congratulations, Doctor. That was a beautiful speech yesterday."

I said: "Thank you. I'm very flattered."

He said: "Doctor, tonight we're having a Sports Celebrity Banquet at your hotel. Why don't you come?"

I said: "I'd love to."

Jo looked at me with astonishment. She said: "We're all supposed to have dinner tonight at your sister's house. She's been preparing for it all week."

"That's right," I said, remembering. "I'm sorry. We're committed."

He said: "Let's leave it at this. I'll have a table reserved for you. If you can make it, fine. Bring along as many people as you like."

"Okay. Thanks."

The next item on the agenda was a private tour of the White House for the whole family. The women loved the paintings of the First Ladies and the dining rooms, all laid out with beautiful silver and gorgeous table linen. At one point, we had to go up some stairs, which I couldn't do, so my son James and I and a Secret Service man used the elevator in the kitchen. On the way up, we passed the First Family's living quarters and I saw a baby buggy in the hall, probably belonging to the Carters' new grandchild. It was a moment of insight into the Carter family that was warm and loving, something that touched me.

That afternoon, as we were driving out to my sister's house in Virginia, Jo said: "I'm going to ask Lucretia to have an early dinner so that you and the boys can go to that banquet tonight. I know how much you want to go."

"That would be nice," I said, "but maybe we shouldn't eat and run."

My sister understood. Dinner was early. After it, we were all out on the patio, having a drink, and I had just about given up on the banquet. Suddenly a storm struck and the electrical power in the neighborhood went dead.

Jo said: "There's your answer. There's no sense sitting around in the dark. Go to the banquet."

I asked: "What about you? What are you and the girls going to do for the evening?"

"We'll figure out something. Take the boys and go to the banquet. I'll see you at the hotel later."

I didn't need any further persuasion.

The banquet was wonderful. I had never seen so many famous athletes in one place at the same time. When the proceedings began and Keith Jackson, the sportscaster, started making introductions, each athlete received an ovation. I wanted to stand up and applaud them, too, but I couldn't, so I applauded them with my admiration and respect.

Suddenly I heard Keith say my name. With that, a spotlight was focused on me. Keith talked about the presidential award, my work, my speech, and he referred to me as a "champion of champions." Another standing ovation. I was so surprised, so overwhelmed, that I got all choked up, and I was glad I was not expected to say anything. Men came to the table to congratulate me. Women came over and kissed me.

Jo and the girls arrived just as the banquet was breaking up. Jo asked: "Did you have a good time?"

"Oh, yes," I said. "I had a wonderful time."

James said: "A lot of women came over and kissed Daddy."

Jo sent me a studied look, but then Joseph explained what had happened. Jo beamed and said: "Aren't you glad you came? And now I wonder how we're going to be able to live with you after all this."

Just about this time I was notified by St. Francis College that my alma mater wanted to present me with an honorary doctorate in science at the 1977 commencement exercises in June. This was completely unexpected, almost as remote as the presidential award. I was very flattered.

The exercises were held in the Brooklyn Academy of Music, Brooklyn's answer to Carnegie Hall. As I sat there on the stage that day, I realized that this was the third degree I would receive in this auditorium. The first was in 1942 when, as a graduate of St. Francis, I received my bachelor's degree, *cum laude*. I remembered how proudly, how firmly, I had walked down the aisle that day. The second time was in 1945, when I walked down the aisle to receive my medical degree from Long Island Medical College. That time I was proud in my walk but not so firm. The first symptoms of my multiple sclerosis had appeared, and I had to be careful about how I walked. And now, in 1977, there I was up on the stage in my wheelchair.

When the time came for the presentation, Brother Donald Sullivan, the president of the college, began to read the citation. It was so full of accolades about me and my work that I became embarrassed.

I whispered to Jo: "Who is he talking about?"

She said: "I don't know. But I'm sure if I knew that man I would love him and I could be very happy with him."

Indeed, among all men I was truly blest.

And I was aware that any disabled person could be equally blessed as long as he was surrounded by that much love, as long as he was given that much encouragement to win the battle against himself. But there had to be something else involved. In one way or another, all of us handicapped people have stiffened arms, and the only way we can create our own heavens here on earth is, first of all, to start feeding others.

Years ago, I heard Dr. Howard Rusk say: "We must do all we can to help the disabled learn that arms and legs and eyes and ears don't make the man. Spirit makes the man."

It is a spirit that God gives us all.

Appendix

PEOPLE WITH DISABILITIES of any kind have countless opportunities in this country for patient care, personal assistance and job training. You can find out about services offered at the federal level by writing the Department of Health, Education and Welfare in Washington, D.C. Usually the federal programs are administered at the state and county levels, and you can find out about them at your county health department. Your doctor will probably know about them, too.

There are also many eleemosynary organizations that raise money for research and patient care for just about every ailment there is—multiple sclerosis, muscular dystrophy, cerebral palsy, blindness, cancer, polio, heart conditions and on and on. These organizations often function at the county level; and you can find out about them at your county health department, from your local newspaper or your telephone directory.

And across the country are hundreds of rehabilitation facilities with excellent equipment and qualified professional staffs. Following is a list of some of them, culled from the annual directory of the Association of Rehabilitation Facilities and presented here with the association's permission. First is a list of the services offered, identified by letters of the alphabet. Then comes the list itself, with the services of each facility indicated by letters of the alphabet. This is by no means a complete list, nor is it a recommended list; but if the facility nearest you doesn't have the services you need, they can direct you to others that do.

PROGRAM SERVICES CODING

Small Letters: Services submitted in rank order.

Capital Letters: Services not rank ordered and appear in alphabetical order.

When Left Blank: Information on request

PROGRAM SERVICES AND OTHER SERVICES

a Developmental
b Physical Restoration
c Psycho/Social
d Speech/Pathology Audiology
e Vocational/Educational
f Work Activity
g Alcoholism
h Blind
i Community Education (includes continuing education, remediation and driving)
j Deaf/Blind
k Deaf Education
l Drug and/or Alcohol
m Evaluation and Adjustment
n Extended Employment
o Geriatric Services
p Learning Disabilities
q Occupational Therapy
r Placement
s Preschool day care
t Recreation (includes adult activities, camping, day care)
u Residential (includes group homes)
v Sheltered Employment
w Sheltered Workshop
x Visually Impaired
y Vocational Adjustment
z Vocational Evaluation

ALABAMA

Huntsville Rehabilitation Center
316 Longwood Drive, S.W.
Huntsville, Alabama 35801
(205) 534-6421
Carl L. Shreve, Administrator
Services, w/e/b/d

Central Alabama Rehabilitation Center
2125 East South Boulevard
Montgomery, Alabama 36116
(205) 288-0240
Robert E. Jordan, Administrator
Services: e/b+d/c+a

ARIZONA

Arizona Foundation for the Handicapped
4700 North Central
Phoenix, Arizona 85012
(602) 266-6111
Donald J. Hinkel, Executive Director
Services: e/f/v

ARKANSAS

Hot Springs Rehabilitation Center
P.O. Box 1358
Hot Springs, Arkansas 71901
(501) 624-4411
Gene Harwood, Administrator
Services: e/b/c/f/d

CALIFORNIA

Redwoods United, Inc.
1611 Samoa Road, P.O. Box 1400
Eureka, California 95501
(707) 443-0811
Leon Berliner, Executive Director
Services: E/F

St. Jude Hospital and Rehabilitation Center
101 East Valencia Mesa Drive
P.O. Box 4138
Fullerton, California 02634
(714) 871-3280
Francis G. Mackey, Medical Director
Services: b/d

Casa Colina Hospital for Rehabilitative Medicine
255 East Bonita Avenue
Pomona, California 91767
(714) 593-7521
Dale E. Eazell, President
Services: b/a/e/f/d/u

San Francisco Community Rehabilitation Workshop, Inc.
P.O. Box 11255
(191 8th Street)
San Francisco, California 94101
(415) 431-9200
Randall V. Frakes, Executive Director
Services: E

Rancho Los Amigos Hospital
12924 Juniper Street
Downey, California 90242

COLORADO

Four Corners Sheltered Workshops, Inc.
3121 Main Avenue, P.O. Box 1778
Durango, Colorado 81301
(303) 247-0277
Allen Jones, Executive Director
Services: A/E/F

CONNECTICUT

Easter Seal Rehabilitation Center of Eastern Fairfield
County
226 Mill Hill Avenue
Bridgeport, Connecticut 06610

(203) 366-7551
Edmund S. McLaughlin, Executive Director
Services: b/d/a

HARTFORD EASTER SEAL REHABILITATION CENTER
80 Coventry Street
Hartford, Connecticut 06112
(203) 243-9741
June Sokolov, Director
Services: b+e/c/a/d

DELAWARE

DELAWARE CURATIVE WORKSHOP
1600 Washington Street
Wilmington, Delaware 19802
(302) 656-2521
Mae D. Hightower, Executive Director
Services: b/d/a/e/c

DISTRICT OF COLUMBIA

VOCATIONAL ADJUSTMENT CLINIC
1717 Rhode Island Avenue, N.W.
Washington, D.C. 20036
(202) 347-1295
John Daugherty, Director
Services: e/f/c

FLORIDA

PALM BEACH HABILITATION CENTER, INC.
4522 South Congress Avenue, P.O. Box 631
Lake Worth, Florida 32460
(305) 965-8500
Robert R. Benedict, Executive Director
Services: A/C/E/U/W

GOODWILL INDUSTRIES SUNCOAST, INC.
P.O. Box 14456
St. Petersburg, Florida 33733
(813) 576-3819
James J. Szenas, President
Services: v/e/c

GEORGIA

GEORGIA REHABILITATION CENTER
Warm Springs, Georgia 31830
(404) 655-3341
Robert M. Long, Director
Services: e/c/a/y/b/d

GEORGIA WARM SPRINGS HOSPITAL
Warm Springs, Georgia 31830
(404) 655-3321
T. S. Oglesby, Acting Director
Services: B

HAWAII

REHABILITATION HOSPITAL OF THE PACIFIC
226 North Kuakini Street
Honolulu, Hawaii 96817
(808) 531-3511
Charles R. Yarbrough, Vice President
Services: b/d

IDAHO

IDAHO ELKS REHABILITATION HOSPITAL
204 Fort Place
Boise, Idaho 83702
(208) 343-2583
Richard L. Williams, Administrator
Services: B

WESTERN IDAHO TRAINING COMPANY
819 4th Avenue North
Nampa, Idaho 83651
(208) 467-3318
Robert N. Jarboe, Executive Director
Services: e/a

ILLINOIS

JEWISH VOCATIONAL SERVICE AND EMPLOYMENT CENTER
1 South Franklin Street
Chicago, Illinois 60606
(312) 356-6700
William Gellman, Executive Director
Services: E

SCHWAB REHABILITATION HOSPITAL
1401 South California Boulevard
Chicago, Illinois 60608
(312) 522-2010
Murray Berg, Executive Director
Services: B/C/D/E

INSTITUTE OF PHYSICAL MEDICINE AND REHABILITATION
619 N. E. Glen Oak Avenue
Peoria, Illinois 61603
(309) 676-8706
Rex O. McMorris, Executive Director
Services: b/c/e/d

INDIANA

THE REHABILITATION CENTER, INC.
3701 Bellemeade Avenue
Evansville, Indiana 47715
(812) 479-1411
Lee Baker, Executive Director
Services: b/d/a/c/e

TRADE WINDS REHABILITATION CENTER
5901 West Seventh Avenue
Gary, Indiana 46406
(219) 949-4000
Franklin M. Rosenbaum, Executive Director
Services: b/d/a/e/c

CROSSROADS REHABILITATION CENTER
3242 Sutherland Avenue
Indianapolis, Indiana 46205
(317) 924-3251
John J. Christy, Executive Director
Services: e/w/b/k/a/d/c

BONA VISTA PROGRAMS
1220 East Laguna Street
Kokomo, Indiana 46901
(317) 457-8286
Paul F. Wagner, Jr., Executive Director
Services: e/a/f/d/u

KANSAS

KANSAS ELKS TRAINING CENTER FOR THE HANDICAPPED
619 South Maize Road
Wichita, Kansas 67209
(316) 722-1551
Dean B. Settle, Executive Director
Services: e/f/a/c

KENTUCKY

CARDINAL HILL HOSPITAL
2050 Versailles Road
Lexington, Kentucky 40504
(606) 254-5701
Robert A. Silvanik, Executive Director
Services: b/e/a/c/d

INSTITUTE OF PHYSICAL MEDICINE AND REHABILITATION, INC.
220 Abraham Flexner Way
Louisville, Kentucky 40202

(502) 582-2231
Robert W. Wiesman, Administrator
Services: b

LOUISIANA

DELGADO REHABILITATION CENTER
615 City Park Avenue
New Orleans, Louisiana 70119
(504) 482-5448
Douglas Wells, Director
Services: E

MAINE

BANGOR REGIONAL REHABILITATION CENTER
P.O. Box 861
Bangor, Maine 04401
(207) 947-6523
Philip E. Ward, Jr., Executive Director
Services: e/f/a

MARYLAND

DEPARTMENT OF REHABILITATION MEDICINE—SINAI HOSPITAL
Belvedere Avenue at Greenspring
Baltimore, Maryland 21215
(301) 367-7800
Bernard H. Suffel, Administrative Coordinator
Services: b/e/c/d/f

MASSACHUSETTS

REHABILITATION INSTITUTE—NEW ENGLAND MEDICAL CENTER
   HOSPITAL
185 Harrison Avenue
Boston, Massachusetts 02111
(617) 956-5625
James F. Holzer, Departmental Administrator
Services: b+d/e+c

MICHIGAN

League for the Handicapped Goodwill Industries
1401 Ash Street
Detroit, Michigan 48208
(313) 964-3900
Russell G. Albrecht, President
Services: e/c/f/a

MINNESOTA

Multi Resource Centers, Inc.
1900 Chicago Avenue South
Minneapolis, Minnesota 55404
(612) 871-2402
R. W. Will, President
Services: c/e

Sister Kenny Institute
27th Street & Chicago Avenue
Minneapolis, Minnesota 55407
(612) 874-4463
Albert P. Calli, Executive Director
Services: B/C/D/E

NEW HAMPSHIRE

Crotched Mountain Rehabilitation
Greenfield, New Hampshire 03047
(603) 547-3311
Joseph S. Handy, Executive Director
Services: e/b/c/d/a/f

NEW JERSEY

Kessler Institute for Rehabilitation
Pleasant Valley Way
West Orange, New Jersey 07052
(201) 731-3600
William K. Page, Executive Director
Services: b/c+d/e

NEW MEXICO

THE REHABILITATION CENTER
1023 Stanford Drive, N.E.
Albuquerque, New Mexico 87106
(505) 255-5501
Duane S. Hill, Executive Director
Services: b+e/f/d/c

NEW YORK

UNITED CEREBRAL PALSY OF QUEENS
81-15 164th Street
Jamaica, New York 11432
(212) 380-3000
Daniel Wieder, Executive Director
Services: e/c/f/a

ALTRO HEALTH AND REHABILITATION SERVICES
225 Park Avenue South
New York, New York 10003
(212) 684-0600
Harold M. Kase, Executive Vice President
Services: c/e/f

BELLEVUE HOSPITAL
27th Street and First Avenue
New York, New York 10016
(212) 561-3601
Bruce B. Grynbaum, Director of Rehabilitation Medicine
Services: b/c/e/d

Brunswick Hospital Center
Rehabilitation Hospital
366 Broadway
Amityville, New York 11701
(516) AM4-5000
Joseph J. Panzarella, Jr., M.D., Medical Director
Services: b/c/d/g/l/o/q

FEDERATION EMPLOYMENT AND GUIDANCE SERVICES
28 East 21st Street
New York, New York 10010
(212) 777-4900
Alfred P. Miller, Executive Director
Services: e/f/a/c

FEDERATION OF THE HANDICAPPED
211 West 14th Street
New York, New York 10011
(212) 242-9050
Milton Cohen, Executive Director
Services: e/f/c

FOUNTAIN HOUSE, INC.
425 West 47th Street
New York, New York 10036
(212) 582-0340
John H. Beard, Executive Director
Services: c/e

ICD REHABILITATION AND RESEARCH CENTER
340 East 24th Street
New York, New York 10010
(212) 697-0100
James C. Folsom, Director
Services: e/c/d/b

INSTITUTE OF REHABILITATIVE MEDICINE
400 East 34th Street
New York, New York 10016
(212) 679-3200
George De Graff, Administrator
Services: b/e+c/f+d

SHELTERED WORKSHOP OF BIRD S. COLER HOSPITAL
Roosevelt Island
New York, New York 10044
(212) 688-9400
Perry M. Rattiner, Chief Vocational Rehabilitation Counseling
Services: b

UNITED CEREBRAL PALSY OF NEW YORK CITY
122 East 23rd Street
New York, New York 10010
(212) 677-7400
Jerry Rubino, Director of Vocational Services
Services: f/e/c/a

ROCHESTER REHABILITATION CENTER
1000 Elmwood Avenue
Rochester, New York 14620
(716) 442-4100
Earl W. Fahy, Executive Director
Services: e/f/c/i+u/b

SUNNYVIEW HOSPITAL AND REHABILITATION CENTER
1270 Belmont Avenue
Schenectady, New York 12308
(518) 382-4500
Robert E. Ward, President
Services: b/d/e

CONSOLIDATED INDUSTRIES OF GREATER SYRACUSE, INC.
541 Seymour Street
Syracuse, New York 13204
(315) 476-4021
Allen Speiser, Executive Director
Services: C/E/F/W

BURKE REHABILITATION CENTER
785 Mamaroneck Avenue
White Plains, New York 10605
(914) 958-0050
William D. O'Connor, Associate Executive Director
Services: b/e+c/d

NORTH CAROLINA

CHARLOTTE REHABILITATION HOSPITAL
1100 Blythe Boulevard
Charlotte, North Carolina 28203
(704) 333-6634
J. Patrick Thompson, Administrator
Services: b/e/c+d

NORTH DAKOTA

MEDICAL CENTER REHABILITATION HOSPITAL
P.O. Box 8202, University Station
Grand Forks, North Dakota 58201
(701) 772-8141
Kenneth W. Aitchison, Administrator
Services: b/c/e/d

OHIO

JEWISH VOCATIONAL SERVICE
1660 Sternblock Lane
Cincinnati, Ohio 45237
(513) 631-2400
Bernard S. Rosenthal, Executive Director
Services: E/F

VOCATIONAL GUIDANCE AND REHABILITATION SERVICE
2239 East 55th Street
Cleveland, Ohio 44103
(216) 431-7800
Theodore Fabyan
Services: e/c/b

OHIO STATE UNIVERSITY HOSPITAL'S DODD HALL
472 West 8th Avenue
Columbus, Ohio 43210
(614) 422-5547
Dale H. Rogers, Administrator
Services: B

GOOD SAMARITAN MEDICAL CENTER PHYSICAL MEDICINE AND
    REHABILITATION CENTER
800 Forest Avenue
Zanesville, Ohio 43701
(614) 454-5000
Mary G. Swope, Executive Director
Services: b/d

BRYN MAWR HOSPITAL REHABILITATION CENTER
Malvern, Pennsylvania 19355
(215) 647-3150
Thomas M. Nojunas, Administrator
Services: B

MAGEE MEMORIAL REHABILITATION CENTER
1513 Race Street
Philadelphia, Pennsylvania 19102
(215) 864-7100
Joseph A. Rainville, 3rd, Vice President
Services: b/d/c/e/z

HARMARVILLE REHABILITATION CENTER
Guys Run Road, P.O. Box 11460
Pittsburgh, Pennsylvania 15238
(412) 781-5700
Lee H. Lacey, President
Services: b/e/c/d

HOME FOR CRIPPLED CHILDREN
1426 Denniston Avenue
Pittsburgh, Pennsylvania 15217
(412) 521-9000
Charles H. Bisdee, President
Services: A/B/C/D/E/F

DEPARTMENT OF REHABILITATION MEDICINE ST. FRANCIS GENERAL
   HOSPITAL
45th Street
Pittsburgh, Pennsylvania 15201
(412) 622-4302
Joseph Novak, Medical Director
Services: b

THRESHOLD OF BERKS COUNTY, INC.
405 Pennsylvania Street
Reading, Pennsylvania 19601
(215) 374-8257
John H. Moore, Jr., Executive Director
Services: e/c

ALLIED SERVICES FOR THE HANDICAPPED
475 Morgan Highway
Scranton, Pennsylvania 18508
(717) 346-8411
George T. Walters, President

RHODE ISLAND

VOCATIONAL RESOURCES, INC.
100 Houghton Street, P.O. Box 6663
Providence, Rhode Island 02940
(401) 861-2080
Eleanor O. Seaman, Executive Director
Services: e/c/f

TEXAS

WEST TEXAS REHABILITATION CENTER
4601 Hartford Street
Abilene, Texas 79605
(915) 692-1633
Shelley V. Smith, Executive Director
Services: b/d/g/e/c/a

DALLAS REHABILITATION INSTITUTE
7850 Brookhollow Road
Dallas, Texas 75235
(214) 637-0740
Raymond L. Dabney, Executive Director
Services: b/f/e/c/d

TEXAS INSTITUTE FOR REHABILITATION AND RESEARCH
1333 Moursund Avenue
Houston, Texas 77025
(713) 797-1440
William A. Spencer, President
Services: b/e/c/f

GOODWILL REHABILITATION SERVICE
P.O. Box 21340
San Antonio, Texas 78221

(512) 923-7793
A. J. Bob Blase, Executive Director
Services: e

INDIVIDUAL DEVELOPMENT CENTER
3401 Armory Road
Wichita Falls, Texas 76302
(817) 766-3207
Richard F. Weber, Executive Director
Services: e/z/c

VIRGINIA

SHELTERED OCCUPATIONAL CENTER OF NORTHERN VIRGINIA
4214 North 9th Street
Arlington, Virginia 22203
(703) 524-6161
Richard M. Valentine, Executive Director
Services: A/F

DEPARTMENT OF VOCATIONAL REHABILITATION WOODROW WILSON
    REHABILITATION CENTER
Fishersville, Virginia 22939
(703) 885-7281
J. Ellies Moran, Director
Services: b/e/z/c/f/d/a

WASHINGTON

UNIVERSITY HOSPITAL DEPARTMENT OF REHABILITATION MEDICINE
1959 N. E. Pacific Street
Seattle, Washington 98195
(206) 543-3600
Justus Lehmann, Professor and Chairman

WEST VIRGINIA

WEST VIRGINIA REHABILITATION CENTER
Barron Drive
Institute, West Virginia 25112
(304) 768-8861
George F. Gay, Administrator
Services: e/f/b/a/d/c

WISCONSIN

CURATIVE WORKSHOP OF GREEN BAY
342 South Webster Avenue
Green Bay, Wisconsin 54301
(414) 435-3721
William K. Nystrom, Executive Director
Services: e/a/b/w/c/f/d

CURATIVE WORKSHOP OF MILWAUKEE
9001 West Watertown Plank Road
Milwaukee, Wisconsin 53226
(414) 259-1414
Eugene M. Cox, Executive Director
Services: b/e/a/f/c/d

JEWISH VOCATIONAL SERVICE
1339 North Milwaukee Street
Milwaukee, Wisconsin 53202
(414) 272-1344
Michael M. Galazan, Executive Director
Services: C/D/E/F/O

CANADA

JEWISH VOCATIONAL SERVICE OF METROPOLITAN TORONTO
74 Tycos Drive
Toronto, Ontario, Canada M6B IV9
(416) 787-1151
Milton Friedman, Executive Director
Services: e/c

G. F. STRONG REHABILITATION CENTRE
4255 Laurel Street
Vancouver, B.C., Canada V5Z 2G9
(604) 734-1313
E. J. Desjardins, Manager
Services: B

T